LESSONS LEARNED WITHOUT A SCHOOL

The book you wish you'd had
when life hit the fan

STEPHEN SCOTT

For Daisy, Molly, Annie,

and my best friend for over 30 years, Jean.

CONTENTS

AUTHOR'S NOTE

Final School Report for
Stephen Scott, February 1983

"I left Stephen's report until last, as during my teaching career I have never found it so difficult to write anything good about a pupil and in this case, I failed miserably. I have not known him to do one positively good thing. He is disruptive, deceitful, untruthful—in fact—amoral. I hope he will change for the good someday soon, for other people's sakes. If he was a good physical specimen, I would be even more worried than I am now. This school is much improved by his absence. He does have intelligence but wastes the gift, generally."

At fifteen years of age, I was permanently expelled from my secondary school for the extremely serious offence of slow-handclapping my headmaster, Mr. Skinner, after one of his rambling speeches in assembly. I wasn't the only pupil who had slow-handclapped Mr. Skinner, nor had I started it, but I was the only pupil called to account. Because I couldn't give a reason as to why I had committed such a heinous crime, Mr. Skinner concluded that I couldn't be trusted, so I was expelled from the school permanently. I was also told that I would not be allowed back onto the school premises again to take my forthcoming exams.

In the report above, my form teacher not only wrote me off as a person, but he assassinated my character. I had long forgotten this report until I stumbled across it in an old shoebox, but when I read those words again from over forty years ago, I feel incredible anger that anyone could write such venomous words about a fifteen-year-old kid who wasn't a criminal, hadn't mugged anyone, hadn't burgled anyone's house or dealt drugs. My only crime was that I had an opinion and voiced it.

During this time, I was extremely outspoken against the UK Prime Minister, Margaret Thatcher, who seemed intent on smashing everything the working class had fought for and was on the verge of taking on Arthur Scargill and the National Union of Mineworkers (NUM) in an orchestrated attack to not only smash the NUM, but unions generally in the UK. In the United States, Ronald Reagan was president, aggressively pushing his trickledown economics theory, which saw huge tax cuts for businesses and the already wealthy in the misguided belief that their increased wealth would be then trickled down to the rest of society. I think history clearly shows this theory doesn't work and the rich tend to hold on to their wealth. So there was a lot for me to be speaking out against in the early 1980s.

The whole school system back then seemed geared toward pushing working-class kids like me down the route of menial work. We were never encouraged to believe we could be anything other than cannon fodder for the system. I, however, had other ideas about what I wanted to do, and I always knew that a lifetime spent on a factory floor would not be my lot. I'm convinced this is what got up the nose of my form teacher, a man in his mid-to-late thirties who seemed to fancy himself as some kind of "hard man" as he strutted around the school amongst us kids. He was one of those teachers pupils feared, and he seemed to revel in this knowledge. But despite commanding a respect born through fear within the school, he also seemed to be someone who liked to try and impose himself physically outside of teaching. I remember he once came into school with his face covered in cuts and bruises. Rumours spread that he had got into a fight in his local pub and obviously came off second best. This was later confirmed as true by a relative of mine who drank in the same pub.

Directly under the report from my form teacher, my headmaster wrote:

"His teachers, without exception, find Stephen difficult, if not downright unpleasant and unteachable. Rarely have I met a youth with such a complex and huge chip on his shoulder, believing that he only is right and everyone else, especially those with a responsibility for him, are wrong."

It is hard to imagine that a teacher could ever get away with writing such damning words these days. Had I been a pupil in today's educational system, and with the societal standards we now have, I might have been diagnosed with some kind of disorder and given help and support. Reading through my old reports, it is clear that I was also going through a crisis, but no one came to help. The crisis itself was probably first brought on by my father leaving the family home when I was eight years old, and then from being at the mercy of my mother's overbearing parenting and paranoia. (More to come on both later in this book).

As I write these words, it is September 9th, 2022—some twenty-one years since the Twin Towers were attacked, and a day after Queen Elizabeth II died, aged ninety-six.

I confess I have never been a monarchist, but I did have a certain respect for the Queen. Everything I have heard about her since her death suggests she was a compassionate, caring, and good person, and that she selflessly did the best she could to serve her nation and its people under what I can only imagine as relentless pressure.

Now, with that out of the way, let's get onto the real point of this book. Writing it has been a stop-start affair which began in May 2021. I kept returning to the manuscript whenever something new came to my mind that I felt compelled to write about. My initial intention was to impart some of the lessons, knowledge, and wisdom that I have accumulated during my journey through life up until this point. Much of the wisdom has been gained from my own mistakes and bad decisions, and it is fair to say these have been lessons learned the hard way.

I want this book to be a comforting arm around the shoulder of the reader, letting them know that they are not alone in feeling how they feel. You may well ask who I think I am to be so pompous as to think I can give out advice and words of wisdom—and I don't blame you, especially when I have personally fucked up more times than I care to remember and continue to do so. But that is exactly the point. The fact that I have fucked up and gone on to learn the lessons from my many fuck ups puts me in a position where I can offer some wisdom from the lessons I have learned. I hope that the honesty and lack of bullshit and ego will make my words relatable to you, the reader. And ultimately, if this book helps, guides, inspires, or comforts just one person through whatever challenges they are experiencing, then the countless hours spent writing it have been worthwhile.

How you read and interpret this book is your choice. You may conclude it to be total bullshit (I hope not), which, as a reader who has spent their hard-earned money, is your absolute right. But please know this one fact: it has been written with honesty and openness. Within these pages, you'll find a man laying bare his soul and admitting to his weaknesses, his failures, and even his crimes. You'll find a man confronting the truths he has failed to confront in the past, and repenting. It is a man letting go of ego and telling his truth, no matter how painful it is to do so.

Maybe if we were all a bit more honest, then the world would be a better place. I don't profess to have the answers to anything. This is simply my story and my truth, presented here for you to read.

Wisdom is something that comes with age. When we are younger, we think we know it all and we feel we already have all the answers and the wisdom we need. No one can tell us anything we don't already know. We casually dismiss old people and sometimes laugh at what they say, believing they know nothing about the world today.

But older people have lived a life. They have made the mistakes you have made (or are about to make), and they have learned lessons by those mistakes. They have known success and failure, they have loved and they have lost. They have, as the saying goes, "done that and got the t-shirt".

The young people of today and of future generations may not want to listen to their elders; it seems that every young generation has this in common. But we would be wise to put our arrogance aside and listen. We dismiss the wisdom and stories of older generations at our peril. The path you are walking has been walked a billion times before, by people who have now departed this earth. To quote the Old Testament of the Bible, Ecclesiastes 1:9, "There is nothing new under the sun."

When we are young, we feel this is the first time anyone has felt as we do, and that no one else understands. We foolishly think we are the first to have ever walked this path, so how could anyone else know what it's like? As I told my daughters when they were younger, "You can't fool me. Whatever you have done, I have done it also, and most probably worse."

For me, this book signals the time for me to be truthful, because being truthful is not something I have always been. I have lied and cheated. I have damaged, hurt, upset, stolen, and deceived. In fact, murder is probably the only amoral thing I haven't done. I am no saint, that is an undeniable fact; but then who walking this earth is? I have been hugely judgmental, rude, ignorant, arrogant, sinful. I have sunk to some of the lowest depths. I have been, in essence, everything that is human. But right now, I am on a journey of redemption and self-improvement. I no longer want to continue being the person I have been.

We all wear a mask, or many masks, and these masks hide our truth. You may think that you yourself don't wear one. Don't be deceived. Like everyone, you wear many masks. The mask you wear at work is different from the mask you wear at home. The mask you wear with friends is different from the mask you wear with your family. Your external shell, with all its clothing and finery, is a mask of how you want to present yourself to the world.

But the real you is the internal voice which speaks to you at night as you lie alone in bed, when the mask is finally off. This internal voice will always tell you the truth, which can be brutal and painful to hear, so we often go into denial and try to change the internal dialogue. We may try to drown it out with alcohol, drugs, sex—anything we can find to silence the truth.

How do I know? I have worn a mask all my life. It has, in my case, been worn in a belief that it will protect me. I have spent years trying to ignore my internal voice. But it has continued screaming at me all this time, wanting to be heard.

Over the last few years, I have become tired of wearing masks and the dishonesty of it all. I am now at the point of taking all those masks off and discarding them for good. However,

I'm learning that after fifty-six years of wearing masks, it is not something you can just do overnight. Writing this book has been part of the journey.

Before now, the only time I ever let my true authentic voice speak was when I wrote songs. Other than that, it was kept locked up and deep within. To keep denying the internal voice is toxic to your body, soul, and mind. It must eventually be heard, and we must all eventually confront the truth it speaks.

This book is my attempt to confront the uncomfortable truths. I never accepted what my form teacher and headmaster wrote in my report back in 1983—they didn't know the real me, they didn't know the absolute drive and passion I had within to be so much more than just another wretched soul churned out by the UK education system, I hope that you will find something in my journey that resonates and helps you on your own journey.

When we are born our internal hard-drive is empty, but the challenges we face and the experiences we collect get added onto the hard-drive throughout our lives. This book contains wisdom that I wish I had known much earlier in my life, had I done so then I may well have saved myself a lot of unnecessary stress, anger and anxiety. This is the book I wish I had access to when I was a teenager, as a twenty-something young man, as a person in their thirties, and even beyond. The lessons in this book are not presented in chronological order, so you can read it cover-to-cover or dip in and out of it as a reference. Read whichever chapter or section shouts out to you most when you pick up the book, and remember you have more people in your corner cheering you on and supporting you than you probably realise.

Steve Scott
SEPTEMBER 2022

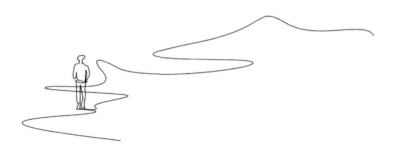

IN THE BEGINNING

So, where do I start?

I guess the natural starting point is at the very beginning of one's own existence. In my case, it began in the mid-60s. I was born in 1966, the year that the England football team won its only World Cup to date, and the same year the Beatles played their last ever live concert at Candlestick Park in San Francisco, USA.

I was brought up in the small town of Selby in the north of England. My parents were young when they had me, and in truth, they were still kids themselves. My mum was only nineteen when she gave birth to me, and my dad had hit twenty a few days before I was born. They were just two kids who had barely started their own life journey, suddenly responsible for another human being. I can only imagine how daunting and scary it must have been for them to become parents so young. I look at my own daughters, who (as I write this) are aged twenty-one and twenty-six, and I cannot imagine them being parents just yet. But as is always the case in life, we deal with whatever curve ball is thrown our way, and we find a way to survive—which is exactly what my parents did.

I was another new life born screaming into the world, and just like everyone else, no matter who their parents are, I was born a wonderfully blank canvas with a whole life ahead of me, filled with possibilities and adventures.

As a baby, I had no concept of any of the things which, as we grow older, begin to weigh us down. I didn't care about how people looked. I had no prejudice against others; I didn't care about skin colour or whether someone was rich or poor. I loved everyone I met. I was here, born into this beautiful world, and I didn't hate anyone or anything. I trusted completely in those who cared for me.

If we think of a newborn baby's brain as a computer hard-drive, when we are born, our hard-drive is completely blank. We have no fears, no worries, no prejudice, and no hatred. But from the moment we are born, our empty hard-drive starts to download the information we see and hear around us. Just watch a baby when you pick it up and start talking to it; the baby will often go quiet and stare at you as they listen to your every word. Already the hard-drive is being filled and programmed.

From the minute you are born to the day you die, the hard-drive is storing information, and this is why we must be mindful of what we say, how we act, and what we expose young minds to. The early years in a child's life are absolutely crucial in the forming of the mind.

If your mind is deviated out of line, even by a little, through a traumatic incident as a child, then by the time you are an adult, if no support has been offered to help you understand and cope with the trauma, it is out of line by a country mile. This huge deviation in later life can manifest itself through mental-health issues, lack of confidence, and behavioral problems. What goes onto the hard-drive in those formative years is vital to how a child will go onto view and approach life in later years. As babies and toddlers, we have no control over what we are exposed to and no control over what goes onto our hard-drive. We are at the complete mercy of those around us.

Please take a minute to think about the great responsibility we have when we bring a child into this world. We know we have to feed, clothe, and protect a child—but what about the mental responsibility we have? What about the responsibilities to ensure we programme the hard-drive with positivity, kindness, and love? In many cases, much of what parents expose their children to is a repeat of what they have installed on their own hard-drive. This is why we can see cycles of experience in so many families. Generations can easily find themselves mirroring the lives of their parents and repeating the same mistakes. Often, it can be tempting to blame everyone and everything else for all our woes, while refusing to take responsibility for how our adult lives are panning out. Remember, this is your life, and no matter what experiences you internalised as a child, it is your responsibility how things play out in adulthood.

Of course, being born into poorer circumstances puts you at a disadvantage from the start. But if you have the drive, desire, and a willingness to work to achieve whatever you dream of and improve your circumstances, then I'm here to tell you that it can be done.

I do not come from anything that can be remotely described as a privileged background. I faced many challenges early on in life. But being born into challenging circumstances doesn't mean that your story—and your destiny—cannot change. There are people who recognise that there is something more out there, and that what they have here and now doesn't have to be their lot. Within some of us is a fighter, who defiantly says, "NO. I will not accept the expected." I consider myself one of these people.

My parents didn't have the long, happy marriage which I

know my mother had hoped for. They split up when I was eight years old. This happened in the early 70s, when single parents were still largely frowned upon by society. The attitude back then encouraged staying married regardless of what went on. Women were expected to put up with their men drinking, coming home drunk, and even having affairs. After all, the men went out and worked hard all week and needed to let off a little steam at the end of the week, didn't they? This seemed to be the attitude at the time, and having divorced parents was not commonplace.

After my parents separated, my dad left home to go and live with his girlfriend. She was eighteen, some ten years younger than he was at the time. One minute, I had a dad at home and a seemingly normal family life. Then, in the blink of an eye, he was gone and my world seemed to fall apart around me. Suddenly, I could only see my dad on the weekends at his parents' house. As a child, I eagerly awaited these weekends that I would get to spend with my dad.

Being a young child from a broken home was uncommon. I certainly wasn't aware of any other kids at my school whose parents were separated, and it wasn't something that was readily spoken of. Thankfully, today we live in much more enlightened times, where the trauma a divorce can have on children is recognised and there are people and organisations out there that can help children get through a family breakup. But back then, I was just expected to get on with it all and live with the consequences. No one ever asked how I was feeling. No help was offered. I was alone and had to deal with the trauma and pain of it all on my own.

I remember crying a lot in the beginning because all I wanted was my mum and dad back together. I prayed a lot, too, even though I wasn't brought up in a religious family. On my birthday, instead of wishing for a new bike or the latest toys, I wished that my mum and dad would get back together. But they never did. As a child, your world revolves around a handful of people, mainly family members. Having that family-oriented world, and the certainty and security it brings, broken up overnight at a young age is devastating. Looking back now, at the age of fifty-five, I can see the enormous effect it had on me—something which I have only recently begun to understand and comprehend. My parents' divorce destroyed my trust and confidence in the world, and was probably the reason for much—if not all—of my anger at any kind of authority as I grew up.

To protect myself from ever being hurt again, I began to build a mental wall around myself to hide my vulnerabilities and shield myself from any form of emotional attack. To the outside world, I appeared hard and uncaring. The parents of my peers labelled me as "trouble", and warned their children to stay clear of me. All the while, I desperately wanted to be loved and feel secure. There is a line from a song by Billy Bragg called "Little Time Bomb," which perfectly sums up where I was throughout my teens and early twenties:

In public he's such a man
And he's punching at the walls with his bare and bloody hands
He's screaming and shouting and acting crazy
But at home he sits alone and he cries like a baby.

My dad leaving home changed everything. It installed on my hard-drive many things, the biggest being insecurity, which is something I will continue to struggle and battle with until the day I die. If my dad could leave me, then how secure was anything in the world? How could I ever trust anyone to not just upsticks and leave? It occurred to me that all of the things I had grown up with, taken for granted, and trusted could be lost in an instant. This made me question my worthiness to be loved. Was I even worthy of anything? It didn't feel like I was.

This was the content on my hard-drive as a child. Events like these get stored internally and create issues further down the line, which we will have to address and understand to be able to move on.

Having a child is a privilege and a huge responsibility, so ensure that you surround your child with love, kindness, and positivity. Be mindful what you say, even when watching the news. Be mindful of making throwaway comments about people. Children hear what you say and store it. Let your children know just how loved they are, and don't be afraid or embarrassed to tell them you love them. Tell them how important and unique they are.

Instill in them a belief that they can be whatever they want to be. Tell them that they can go anywhere, achieve anything, and live the most extraordinary, fulfilling lives.

PROCRASTINATION

As humans, we are fantastic at procrastinating. When we procrastinate, it is usually to avoid something that we perceive to be hard work, or something we find uncomfortable. I started writing this book with the intention to diligently write every day until it was finished. But like a lot of people, I can be prone to laziness, and I will happily find all manner of excuses to not do the hard work. I will actively seek out all manner of non-urgent things to capture my attention and I will kid myself that they simply cannot wait, all so that I can put off what I should be doing—which is writing.

Just today I found myself the victim of procrastination again. I got home from travelling, a journey that involved a 200-mile round trip. On my drive home, I had promised myself that when I got in, I would go straight to my home gym and train, no matter how tired I was feeling. When I did arrive home, instead of going straight into the gym, I decided I needed to eat first, even though I wasn't starving and could quite easily have trained without eating. So that was Procrastination Number One.

After eating, I thought that I shouldn't train straight after food, as it would make me feel sick. Instead, I lay on the bed and got caught up in the world of social media, scrolling through endless, mind-numbing garbage, which led me to doze off. Procrastination Number Two.

When I did eventually wake up, I managed to drag my sorry arse into the gym—some three hours after arriving home. I knew that once I warmed up and got the first few sets out of the way, I would feel more motivated, and the training wouldn't be the chore I had envisaged in my mind.

This example illustrates the problem that I tend to find with a lot of people. They want to achieve something, be someone, go on an adventure—but they don't want to do the hard work. As a trainer and mentor, I have heard every excuse under the sun for not doing the work needed to achieve something my client's desire:

I want to be slim, but I don't want to have to give up cake and sweets.

I want to have a muscular body, but lifting weights is too much like hard work.

Excuses like these also exist outside the realm of training, and prevent us from achieving our goals:

I want to travel the world and have adventures, but I can't be bothered to do all the planning. It's a lot of hassle sorting out visas, accommodation, flights, etc.

I want to write a book but it's hard work. It involves a lot of concentration and just takes too long to finish.

The excuse about writing a book was me for a long time.

For years I've wanted to write a book. In fact, I have started writing many books over the years, and after many enthusiastic starts, my enthusiasm always stopped after a few pages of writing. I had the ideas and stories in my head, but I never wanted to do the hard work of putting those great ideas and stories onto paper. They do say that everyone has got a book within them. Well, mine remained within me for years—due to procrastination.

In years gone by, I was a songwriter, and I recorded and released two records in the late 1980s. Part of the reason I chose songwriting was because writing a song was a relatively easy and quick task for me. I could have one finished (or at least the majority of one finished) within a few hours, or even minutes. I could also say everything I needed and wanted to say in a just a couple of verses and a chorus. Writing a song seemed incredibly natural and easy for me, and even today, if I choose to take myself into the frequency of writing a song I can still do so. I would always be somewhat surprised when I learned that other people I knew and spoke to about writing songs never had tunes just pop into their heads as I did. So, despite wanting to write a great novel, I always took the easy option, which for me was writing songs.

We all procrastinate. We dream of becoming that great vision we have of ourselves in our heads: the great writer, the great business entrepreneur, the person with a great body. But for most people, it remains just a dream. A thought. A desire. It is a "Maybe one day, when I have the time and when things are right for me."

In his book *The Farther Reaches of Human Nature*, American psychologist Abraham Maslow wrote: "We are generally afraid to become that which we glimpse in our most perfect moments, under conditions of great courage. We enjoy and even thrill to godlike possibilities we see in ourselves in such peak moments."

I find the reasons—and the somewhat weak excuses—people give for not pursuing their dreams incredibly sad. The mythical "perfect time" to pursue the dream never seems to come around. There is always another reason why now is not the right time. In truth, now is the perfect time.

Right now, as you are thinking those great ideas and having those great dreams, is the right time. Stop procrastinating and start doing the work, or risk a lifetime of regrets. You don't want to be lying on your deathbed thinking about what might have been and wishing you had done the things you dreamed of. The graveyard is full of people with broken dreams. So even if it's just putting ideas and thoughts down on paper for now, that is a start.

In fact, I urge you to do it now. Pick up a pen and paper and write those dreams down. Otherwise, they will forever remain just thoughts, ideas, and ambitions trapped inside your head, going nowhere. By writing them down, they start to become something real once they are born onto paper. Once written, I urge you to keep reading them as a reminder of your goals, until you have achieved what you wrote down.

My own experiences have taught me that you can achieve pretty much whatever you truly want to achieve—if you are prepared to do the work. The killer of so many dreams is allowing negative thoughts and internal voices to take over your thinking, convincing you that something isn't possible. These negative voices, if allowed to run free unchallenged, will endlessly question and mock you, asking, who do you think you are to have such dreams? They will tell you to be thankful for what you've got and they will warn you not to be greedy and seek to get above your station in life. This toxic drip, drip, drip of self-inflicted negativity will eventually wear you down so much that it sets your plans, hopes, and desires adrift on the overflowing sea of broken dreams. You will end up settling, but within you there will still be an unfulfilled void and an inner voice that rises up and taunts you when you are alone at night with your thoughts. It will whisper, "What if?" and "If only..."

There are excuses by the truckload to be found if you want them. The classics we have all heard at some point are the following:

I'm too old.

I've got a mortgage, so can't take risks.

I'm not fit enough.

I don't have the money.

It's not the right time.

NOW is the exactly the right time. The very fact you have had a moment of inspiration is the Universe telling you to get off your arse and start making it happen. This is your life, your dream, your desire and therefore your responsibility. No one is going to do it for you. No magical hand is going to appear out of the sky, holding a golden platter, saying, "Here you go. Here are those dreams you ordered, just help yourself." Making dreams a reality entails hard work, and it's all part of the journey. If it were easy, everyone would be doing it. It's not meant to be easy.

Every journey starts with that first step. The only difference between you, where you are now, and those you perceive as successful is they took that first step. They took that leap of faith and pursued their dreams. By doing the uncomfortable work, they made their dreams a reality. Dear reader, that is the *only* difference. Successful people—I've met a lot of them over the years—tend to be no cleverer than the rest of us. What they have is desire, drive, and an unbreakable belief that they can make things happen. They will not accept that they cannot do something.

On your journey, expect obstacles, expect difficulties, and expect bumps in the road. The urge to procrastinate is one such challenge you will likely face. But don't let anything stop you.

Thomas Edison, an American inventor best known for his creation of the lightbulb, was asked about his failures. He famously replied, "I have not failed 10,000 times—I've successfully found 10,000 ways that will not work."

It is all about interpretation; is the glass half full or half empty to you? When you get knocked down, you can either stay on the floor and bathe in self-pity or you can get back up, try again, and keep fighting. Procrastination is the enemy of all ambition, yet easy to defeat, as it just requires you to get moving, do something that gets you closer to whatever it is you desire.

PHYSICAL STRENGTH AND DETERMINATION

G enetically, I am naturally skinny. For me, putting on weight has always been an incredibly hard thing to do, no matter how much I eat or what I eat. This is a story about my first steps into the world of bodybuilding, and my journey from being a skinny, nine-stone, twenty-something weakling to being nearly fourteen stone with the muscular physique of a Greek god. (Okay, maybe I exaggerated the Greek god bit. But I did go from being an exceptionally skinny kid to having a muscular body.)

I am what is known as a "hard gainer" in bodybuilding circles. This means that because I struggle to put on weight, I also struggle to put on muscle. So I have to eat a lot, and I mean a lot. I also have to consume a lot of protein, which for me as a vegetarian since the age of 19 means plant-based protein. I had always hated being skinny and I dreamed of putting on weight and having a muscular body. For a long time I believed this was beyond my capability due to my inherited genes. After all, my dad was skinny, his dad (my granddad) was skinny, and my mum was very slim. What chance did I have of putting on weight, let alone building a muscular body? It seemed as if being skinny was my genetic inheritance, whether I liked it or not.

But me being me, I decided I wasn't going to just accept my genetic fate. I decided in my late teens that I would give body-building a good fucking go and put some muscle on my body, even if it killed me in the process. With a dogged determination, I started to lift weights, hoping to put a few inches of muscle on my arms, chest, and legs.

At the time, I had no idea about the complexities of bodybuild-ing or what it truly entailed. I bought some mail-order plastic weights, which I filled with water, and began to do some basic exercises like bicep curls and shoulder presses. I didn't know about overtraining or the need to rest the body after a workout. I assumed that if I trained every day, I would inevitably get bigger. But no matter how much I trained, I never seemed to gain muscle. Then, one day, I bought my first bodybuilding magazine, which changed everything for me. I began to read about diet. I learned about eating clean, training less but going heavy on the weights, and crucially but often overlooked, I read about giving your body time to recover. I also learned about the magic powers of protein and its vital role in helping to build muscle.

I absorbed all this information and started to make immediate changes to my training routine. I cleaned up my diet and I bought and consumed protein powders. As I began to put all the pieces of the puzzle together, I started to see my body grow.

Bodybuilding is a complex jigsaw puzzle, and lifting weights is just one element in the process of putting on muscle. If you miss out or neglect even just *one* key element, you will fail to reach your goals. I learned that I needed to be disciplined, to be all in. I couldn't just do the bits of the puzzle I liked and hope that I would get the desired results. I also discovered what would be a game-changer for me in my quest to build muscle: a supplement called creatine, which I immediately incorporated into my diet.

After a few weeks of putting my plan together and sticking to it religiously, I started to see the early results of my hard work. Firstly, I added an inch on my arms and my chest started to fill out. A few more weeks of training passed and my arms got even bigger, my shoulders grew and became defined, and my chest continued to fill out.

It is fair to say that for two decades I completely threw myself into the sport of bodybuilding; I ate, slept, and dreamed of little else. It completely dominated my life. But here's the thing: building a muscular body is hard fucking work. It requires you to be fully committed to the cause, especially when (like me), you are a hard gainer. It requires lifting heavy weights, endlessly eating the right foods, and drinking plenty of fluid. The whole process can be a grind at times, but I was hooked. If I was ever injured and unable to train—and when you are training to the intensity I was, injuries are a common occurrence—I was like a bear with a sore head.

After years of hard work, I reached my peak in my mid-thirties, boasting 16.5-inch biceps and a near 45-inch chest. I weighed in at just short of fourteen stone, and it was pretty much all muscle.

This bodybuilding journey, as do all journeys, started with a thought; a desire to put on weight and muscle. I knew if I was to achieve my goals, I had to do the work, and I couldn't piss about and go about it half-heartedly. If I did, it would remain just a dream. I took that positive first step and committed myself to training regularly, no matter how much—on some occasions—I felt unmotivated and didn't want to. This commitment paid off, and I went on to build a body I was mostly proud of. (That's the thing with bodybuilding; you always feel you can be bigger and better.)

The lesson is simple: do the research, build a plan of action, and do the fucking work.

Start to map out your journey. I cannot emphasise enough how important it is to actually write down your plan. For me, writing down my plan makes it real, it is my contract to myself, it is me showing a commitment to do the work required to achieve my end goal, my dream. It is also my reference point to remind me of the journey and route I need to take.

List all the small goals and milestones you want to accomplish on the way to reaching your final goal.

Back in the days before we had satnav, if you wanted to travel to a place you had never been to before, you would have to get out a roadmap and plan your journey, noting all the roads and any landmarks along the way. You would write these down on a piece of paper and this would be your plan. As there is no time like the present, I urge you to draw up a similar plan now. Put down this book, get out a pen and paper, and start to map out how you plan to get from where you are now to the object of your dreams.

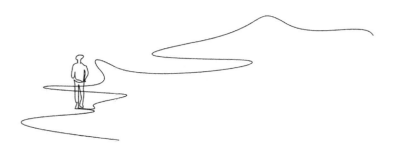

A FAMILY LEGACY

After my dad left our family home when I was eight, he became the classic "weekend father", who I would see every Saturday. We met at my gran and granddad's house on Abbots Road in Selby, North Yorkshire, and we would both stay at their house all day.

Some of my fondest memories of those days involve watching all the big sporting events: the FA cup final (when it really was a big event), the Rugby League Challenge Cup final, the Boat Race, Grand National, the Wimbledon final, and suchlike, with my granddad and my dad. We would all be gathered in the living room shouting at the little TV in the corner of the room, cheering on whichever team we wanted to win. My granddad would tell me stories about all the great sporting teams from the 30s, 40s, and 50s. I would sit listening intently, as he told me tales about footballers such as John Charles, the great Leeds United centre forward who went on to play for the Italian side Juventus, Stanley Matthews, the legendary Stoke and Blackpool player, who even has a Wembley final named after him (the Matthews Final of 1953), and Bert Trautmann, the Manchester City goalkeeper who famously kept on playing after breaking his neck in the

1956 FA Cup Final. When I think back, these are some of my most cherished moments: sitting in the little front room of my grandparents' council house, watching sport, and getting caught up in the drama as it unfolded on the TV.

My gran would go up town on Saturday mornings to do the shopping, and she would come home with comics and sweets for my cousin Shane and I. Then she would make dinner for us all. My favourite was always egg, beans, and chips, with lots of bread and butter. It's still my favourite meal to this day, but no one will ever make it as good as my gran did. I lived for those wonderful Saturdays spent in the company of my dad, granddad, and gran.

Home life with my mum was very different—she hated football and sport generally and when it was on TV would turn the channel over. Conversations with my mum would never involve any talk of sport, or for that matter anything that young boys would normally be interested in. So for a young boy obsessed with football and Leeds United, being around my dad and granddad watching and talking about the things I loved was a refreshing change from life at home with my mum.

During the week, it was just me and my mum, and I was at the mercy of whatever she decided to expose me to. There was no one else around during the week to monitor, control, or challenge what she was putting on my still very young and impressionable internal hard-drive.

What she instilled in me was mainly fear. Complete and utter fear of the world and everyone in it. I was told that everyone was a potential threat. Everyone was a potential murderer or a potential child abuser. She made me so fearful of any stranger that I believed anyone I didn't know was either going to kidnap me, murder me, or do some untold evil to my person. Her constant fear-mongering and warnings had me in a perpetual state of panic and stress whenever I was out in public.

Because of this, I grew up believing that danger and evil lurked around every corner.

Her fears didn't just stop at the threat people posed; she implied that anything I did, such as riding a bike or climbing a tree, could potentially kill me—or at the very least see me seriously injured. As I entered my teens, I started to talk of one day having a motorbike so I could have some freedom, something which is perfectly normal for most boys to dream of. My mother, however, saw motorbikes as a danger which would get me killed, so I was told I wasn't allowed one.

Life with my mother was a constant stream of negativity, though I didn't realise how wrong this was or the harm she was doing to me at the time. I must confess that, today, as an adult and father to two beautiful, vibrant daughters, I still feel some anger at what was done to me by my mother. No matter how well-intentioned it may have been on my mother's part, it had a hugely damaging and negative effect on my life. What she instilled in me was her own paranoia and fears, and in doing so, she was destroying my confidence and trust in the world. Instead of being excited by the wonderful opportunities life had to offer, I was in total fear of it and remained so for many years.

Now, as a father myself, I fully appreciate and understand that children need to be warned of dangers—but not to the extent where they are so filled with fear that it effectively stops them from living. Even to this day, fear is something I still struggle with.

Because of the huge damaging effect her negativity and fear-inducing stories had on me, I have struggled to fully forgive, because I have been the one who has had to live with the consequences of the fear that she instilled in me.

Thankfully, I have always been a fighter. I am not someone

who gives in easily—unless it's DIY. I have always had a deep inner strength that eventually gave me the courage to challenge, rather than just accept what my mother told me. As I got older, I became tired of living in fear, and something within me said, "I won't fucking accept this anymore." So began a lifetime's journey, which has brought me to where I am today.

I am someone who still struggles with fear, but now understands it. Someone who will not let fear dictate and rule his life. I see fear as a challenge, as a motivator, as an enemy to be conquered and defeated. I refuse to let those stories fed to me by my mother have any relevance in my life today.

BULLIES AND TAKING THE
MORAL HIGH GROUND

During your journey through life, you will come across many bullies. The clever ones often don't openly appear to be bullying you, as they do it rather subtly. They may even come across as a friend, while behind the scenes they are stabbing you in the back at every opportunity and undermining you in a passive-aggressive way. To me, this is the worst type of bully. These unseen bullies haven't got the courage to confront you. In fact, when they are in your company, they appear friendly and kind. But behind your back, they are doing their dark, devious, and, frankly, cowardly work, trying to destroy your name. Give me an in-your-face, obvious bully any day of the week over these snakes. Someone getting in your face has a certain honesty about it. Nothing is hidden, and it is easier to deal with and call out. However, those snide, slippery, shit-stirring, behind-your-back, cowardly bastards are harder to deal with.

I am sure you have come across these snakes at some point. Often, they appear in the workplace or in a friend group. They are the ones dropping little "hate bombs" with your name attached into conversations. These individual hate bombs on their own don't do too much damage, but collectively and over time, they can build a completely false narrative and tarnish your reputation, to the extent that people may then think there is something inherently bad or nasty about you—maybe you really aren't someone who can be trusted.

"If you tell a lie big enough and keep repeating it, people will eventually come to believe it," is a quote often attributed to Joseph Goebbels, the German Nazi Party's Head of Propaganda, however there is no evidence that Goebbels did actually say those exact words. The "big lie" theory actually appears to have its origins in Adolf Hitler's book *Mein Kampf*.

So why do some people behave like this?

I'm no psychologist and I don't profess to know what's going on in the minds of these people, but having had them enter my life on occasion, I have a theory. I think they have empty lives, devoid of any real substance, and a hatred of seeing others succeed and be happy. Behind the façade, they have extremely low self-esteem. With minds full of envy, they go about trying to destroy what others have.

Imagine you're out with your friends and one of them mentions that they have heard something unsavoury about you. The rumour is, of course, completely false, so you put the said friend right... but it keeps happening. A single false allegation or story can be relatively harmless if it is confronted and nipped in the bud quickly, but the drip-drip effect involving numerous falsehoods can begin to cast doubt in people's minds about who you really are. Can all these stories just be a coincidence? Your reputation can become questioned and damaged.

When you find out the source of these persistently dropped hate bombs, what can you do? You can go and find the person who started them and deal with them physically. You can go to their house, put the windows through, damage their car, or you could seek revenge in other, equally destructive ways. Thoughts of revenge are perfectly natural. We are all human, and despite efforts to rise above such things, we can all be pushed to a point where we are prone to thoughts of getting even. The test is whether or not you go out and act on those vengeful thoughts, or if you strive to become the better person and rise above such thoughts.

I am not going to give you the answer either way here—that decision is for you and your conscience to decide. I will, however, point out that every action has a reaction, and although your act of revenge may feel good at the time (and even give you some sense of satisfaction after carrying it out), I can tell you from personal experience that once that satisfaction subsides, you will begin to question your actions and ask yourself whether you are actually any better than the people you are taking revenge on.

I believe it is better to take the moral high ground than be dragged down to a bully's level. And I admit, although I say this now, this has not always been my belief, and I have been guilty of going out and seeking revenge in the past.

If you are a good person and do not intentionally go out to cause any harm to anyone, then why should you care what anyone else thinks about you? You know your truth. Whatever bad thoughts others may have about you is surely their problem. You know the lies told about you are not based on any fact. You know that bullies have no real knowledge about you, so why do you care?

Time for a little story.

I once had a neighbour who clearly disliked me. There was no rational reason for this, as I had done him no harm. I had barely even spoken to the guy. In fact, I had gone out of my way to appear friendly, but he never showed any interest in acknowledging this.

Visitors to my house would see the stony-faced glares from him and his equally unfriendly wife and feel uncomfortable. There were even childish, territorial games being played out by the pair of them (particularly the man) in the form of parking his car so it was partially on my property, and placing plant pots over the boundary line onto what was technically my land. But I didn't rise to their silly games and I did my best to ignore them. I remained polite and continued to refuse to take the bait, which I know they both so desperately wanted me to do.

I don't always feel like being polite, and I certainly didn't feel like being polite with this person. If truth be told, I could quite easily and happily have ripped his scrawny little fucking head off, because his behaviour was so awful, abhorrent, and without any justification. Trust me, the option of becoming physical with this pathetic arsehole had crossed my mind many times, and it would have been an incredibly satisfying, easy victory for me. But these days (luckily for him) I am trying to be the better man. I also believe that karma will always catch up with such people. I am aware that, no matter how satisfying it may be to give such arseholes a right-hander, to do so would mean a karmic debt.

So, me and my family continued to ignore the attempts at provocation. We eventually just ignored them as people altogether and got on with our lives, until one day the inevitable showdown happened. One weekend afternoon, the neighbour decided to park his large 4x4 completely on my property, and in the very place where my wife usually parked her car—a fact he knew only too well. As I left the house to go out, I asked him to move his car (politely, of course) as my wife would be returning home shortly. This polite request was his excuse to have the showdown he had been waiting for. With anger in his voice and a twisted face, he began to spew out his perceived grievances, all of which were factually untrue and purely based on his vivid and warped imagination.

Being the nice, restrained person that I am these days, I let him have his irrational rant. I just stood there and observed the anger and stress which was so obviously coursing through his body, causing him immense internal damage in the process. All this vitriol was being vented, but I remained calm. I watched on in amusement as this small-minded man destroyed himself internally before my very eyes. I did not need to become physical, as he was doing a great job of hurting himself. Cuts and bruises will heal very quickly in comparison to the self-inflicted damage my neighbour was causing himself internally.

The lesson here is that people will judge you in life. They will judge you purely on the way you look, sound, or even dress. They will judge you based on your skin colour, hair colour, or even on the car you drive. Some people will judge you without even knowing you. They will make assumptions about the sort of person you are without ever having spoken to you. If you had listened to my neighbour, he would probably paint me as some demon that eats babies for breakfast. But as my wife and children will testify, I am actually someone who will help anyone in need.

During the troubles with my neighbour, the first coronavirus lockdown occurred, in 2020. I went around all the houses on the small estate where I lived at the time and posted notes through the letterboxes of every house on the estate, except that of my awful neighbour. The notes had my contact details and offered to help anyone who needed it with picking up groceries and prescriptions. Hardly the work of a baby-eating monster, is it?

You can be the nicest person on earth, but some people will still dislike you for no discernible reason. You can either spend your time worrying and getting upset about such people, making yourself stressed, unhappy, and sick in the process, or you can choose to think, "Fuck 'em." They are of no importance to you, and their opinion of you is based on nothing factual, as they do not know you.

Bullies do not deserve to occupy any space in your mind whatsoever. To give them any thought and headspace is a victory for them. They want you stressed and angry about them. They want to be living in your head rent-free, caught up in the drama, just like them. Be vigilant, be strong, guard your mind, and don't give them that victory.

In the case of my lovely neighbour, I had clearly been living in his head for months. He had been getting himself worked up over me for no reason whatsoever. After his rude and unwarranted verbal assault, I just thought, "What a prick. Long may I live in your head."

After years of allowing myself to be drawn into futile confrontations, I have learned that, for a confrontation to take place, there must be two willing participants. If one person decides they are not going to play along and become involved in the other person's drama, then it pretty much shuts it down. Without any form of response from you, which they need to justify an escalation in their rage, they implode.

While it isn't a good feeling to think that someone feels so negatively about you, you cannot control the thoughts of other people, so stop trying. My advice is to avoid wasting your thoughts and energy on such people. It is their problem, not yours. Let them continue to stew in the anger and stress of their own making. Let them be the ones to continue to have the sleepless nights and inner rages.

Let them be the ones to suffer from the caustic effects of stress on their body. But above all else, remember that you have a choice. You do not have to become part of someone else's drama. We have no control over what others think, but we do have complete control over how we think and react. As long as they are not physically attacking or abusing you, let them get on with their ridiculous behaviour. Allow yourself a little smile, knowing that their lives must be so empty of real substance and meaning that they have to obsess over you.

THERE'S KARMIC DEBT TO PAY

I'm sure you have heard or read about karma. Probably the most famous iteration of the concept of Karma that you've probably heard is, "What goes around comes around."

Karma, in my understanding, is the absolute truth that whatever you put out into the world returns to you. If you put out hate, you will get hate back. If you are unreasonable, then you cannot expect others to be reasonable to you. If you put out love and kindness, then that is what will be returned to you. Think of karma as looking into a mirror; all your actions are mirrored back to you.

It is important to be mindful of how we go about our lives and our day-to-day dealings with others. One of the lessons I have learned over the years is that everything I do is done of my own free will. I am the one who controls my thoughts and actions. In the past, when I chose to commit crimes, lie, steal, get into fights, get drunk, be abusive, and act like a fucking moron, it was of my own free will. It was my choice and my choice alone. No one held a gun to my head and forced me to do anything. Yes, there are reasons behind why I acted in such ways, but ultimately it was my choice to enact the thoughts I had.

In the past, I have sought to make excuses for the bad behaviour I indulged in, and I have looked to pass the blame anywhere other than where it truly lies—with me. In looking to blame others or to blame my circumstances, I have been trying to con those who know the truth and to con myself into believing I wasn't at fault. Ultimately, I was too weak to admit my own guilt, faults, and failings.

They say that prison is the hardest place to find a guilty man. I have been that man, but who was I trying to kid? Did I really think my crimes would go unnoticed? Everything you do is seen, and every sin and crime committed is witnessed by the Universe. You can deny, lie, and attempt to cover up your crimes in this realm, but you cannot hide them from the higher source. The Universe is keeping score, and one day you will be called to account and answer for your crimes.

Let me just say at this point that this is not me being all God-fearing and evangelical.

This is simply karma, the law of the Universe. It is a fruitless endeavour seeking to deny or cover up your crimes from a Universe that is all-seeing. We need to be strong enough to admit to and own our indiscretions. This will begin the process of healing. It is the first step on the road to redemption, and until we start the process of ownership and taking responsibility for every bad thing we have done, we will remain a prisoner with a karmic debt to pay.

WORKDAYS AS A MEANS TO AN END

My mum always said, "Never burn your bridges, because you never know when you may want to cross them again."

Over the years, I have been guilty of burning many bridges, and it took me a while to fully understand the meaning of this advice and what detriment can befall you if you do not heed it.

Let's look at an example. Say you are leaving a job.

You hate the job, hate the boss, and even dislike most of your colleagues. You have managed to find your new dream job and are working one final day before leaving your old one. You have decided not to leave with a whimper, but with a bang. You're planning to go into the boss's office and tell him what a wanker you think he is and that he can now stick his job where the sun don't shine. (Let's face it, we've all been there. In my case, I've told several bosses what I thought of them.)Because you are leaving, this may seem like a very appealing thing to do, but keep in mind the possible consequences.

5p.m. arrives and you barge into the boss's office, telling him to his face that you think he's a wanker. Then you walk out of his office, giving him the Vs and shouting at the top of your voice, "Stick your fucking job up your arse!" You feel great, you feel empowered, and you are now ready to start your dream job.

Fast-forward to a couple of weeks into the new job, when you begin to realise it isn't exactly the position you were sold. To make matters worse, the new boss is an even bigger wanker than your old boss, and your new colleagues aren't much better. You begin to think that maybe your old job wasn't that bad after all. You have even heard that your old boss has not yet recruited anyone to replace you, and you are starting to wish you hadn't left after all and would like to return.

There is nothing wrong with feeling like that. We all make mistakes and have the right to change our minds. But there is one, rather large problem for you, which makes asking if you can return to your old job a non-starter: you told your old boss you thought he was a wanker and caused quite a scene when you departed. If you had kept your mouth shut and left on amicable terms, you could have contacted your old boss, explained the situation, told him it was a mistake leaving, and asked for your old job back. But your petulant act burnt the bridge, and leaving on bad terms means you are well and truly fucked in the returning department. I'm hoping you are getting the message here, reader.

Make sure you leave anything (and anyone) on as good terms as possible, because you never know when you may need to ask for their help in the future. Remember that whatever you put out returns to you.

It can be hard to imagine returning to a job you hate. My advice is to view a job as a means to an end. Think of it as a temporary fix for the issues and difficulties you may be facing at that time. There is no escaping the fact that we need money to survive. Even while working an awful job, we can still lay the foundations for a new life. There are times in life which require us to make compromises. Problems seem to arise when we see things as being forever. In truth, nothing is forever. Everything eventually moves on if you allow it.

At seventeen, I got my first ever full-time job in a factory making jam. It was a job which, frankly, I found soul-destroying, and had I thought for one minute that it was the job I would be doing for the rest of my life, I would have curled up in a ball and given up there and then. But I knew it wasn't forever, and that it was simply a means to an end. The job was serving the purpose of earning some much-needed money. I knew it was temporary, and I had bigger plans, dreams, and ambitions. For some people who worked at the jam factory, it was a job for life. This was in the mid 80s, at the height of Thatcherism, and jobs were scarce. If you were lucky enough to have a job, you were told to be thankful, not complain, and keep your mouth shut and your head down, no matter how shit and soul-destroying the job was.

A lot of people I speak to about their job seem to view it just as a means to an end. They have no particular love or loyalty to the job. It pays the mortgage and the bills, it puts food on the table, and if they manage to save enough money, it allows them to go on holiday. Some people tell me that they hate their job. When I ask why they stay, they list the reasons above and feel they have no choice.

I now have some questions for you about your job, so get a pen and paper to write down your answers. It is crucial to write your answers down, as it allows you to read back what you have written and review the reasons or excuses (more on that to come). I want you to think seriously about your answers:

1. If you could choose anything in the world to be doing as a job now, what would you choose?
2. What are the reasons why you aren't doing what you

really want to do? What is it you feel is preventing you from doing your dream job?

3. What is stopping you from doing the groundwork to achieve your dream job, even while you are in your present employment? (Be honest!)

Let me tell you the correct answer to the last question: There is no reason why you can't be doing some groundwork right now to achieve your dream job, no matter what your present circumstances are. Any reasons you give are just excuses, and you know that deep inside. I am a firm believer that you can achieve anything you want if you put in the work and really desire it. If you want something badly enough, then you will find a way to make it happen. The issue with a lot of people is that they say they want something, but aren't prepared or willing to do the work. If you don't want to do the work, then you must not want it that badly.

You get to choose whether you remain stuck in the situation you find yourself in right now, or whether you get out of it. We are all free to choose and direct our own lives.

I will repeat that last sentence again, and I want you to absorb and understand how important and empowering it is: We are all free to choose and direct our own lives.

STAND AGAINST HATRED

There are so many people on this earth who are hateful. I myself have been guilty of this at points in my life. I freely admit that I am not perfect, but these days I try to be as perfect as I can be in an imperfect world. As a human, I am fallible and I fail often. When I see myself failing and succumbing to behaviours and thoughts which do not serve me or my goal to being a better human, I try to catch myself and get realigned as quickly as possible. I sometimes fail at this too; when I fail my body can become consumed with such rage and anger that, if I were to let it loose, the consequences of the subsequent explosion would be extremely damaging, not only for those to whom my anger was directed, but also myself. I am a work in progress, and trying to undo over fifty years of habitual behaviour is not easy and is not going to be achieved overnight.

In my younger days, I often found myself walking down the wrong path. Despite knowing in my heart that it was the wrong path, I would carry on walking it for far longer than was good for me, good for the world, or good for those around me. Back then, I was a drinker. When drunk, I would often turn into what I can only describe as a nightmare. A nightmare so unpredictable, that my then girlfriend and future wife has since told me that she used to hate going up town with me on nights out. A sad indictment of the person I was back then, and one which I am determined I will never return to being. I was all too willing to start a fight with anyone who I perceived to have insulted or threatened me. Someone only had to look at me or speak to me in a way I didn't like, and I would see that as an excuse for me to inflict violence upon them. Looking back at the young man I was then, I can see that this was all an act meant to cover up the insecurities and fears I felt. I behaved and acted like an arsehole, and I often found myself in the company of other arseholes. In retrospect, I can see that it was myself I hated.

Inside, I felt massively paranoid and powerless. By being violent and imposing my violence on others, I felt strong and in control. But these were the actions of a man so weak and insecure in himself, that violence was the only thing he felt he had to make himself noticed and heard.

I would often wake up with a huge hangover and tell myself that I would never touch alcohol again. Many times I would wake up without much recollection of what I had done the previous night, other than get drunk. There would only be a sketchy recollection of some altercation. Friends would help me put the jigsaw of the night's events together by recounting what I had done, and I would feel shame and hatred of myself as I learned what they had witnessed. Remorse would then engulf me, and I would make promises to myself that this was to be the last time I would get drunk and violent. Sadly, these would turn out to be empty promises, and the spiral of drunkenness, violence, and self-hatred carried on for a number of years.

Today, the thought of violence sickens me. When I see or hear about it, I feel sadness and anger at the futility of it. However, I do also understand it intimately, and it is this intimate knowledge which allows me to now teach others of its dangers. These days I am a qualified self-defence instructor, teaching pupils how to avoid physical altercations (if possible) and ultimately how to deal with someone who, just like the old me, resorts to violence. I teach about the warning signs and common pre-attack rituals. I teach how to deal with violence should it come calling and present itself in front of you.

While becoming a self-defence instructor and moving forward in life has helped me make peace with my past, violence and hatred is still rampant in society. I see so many people these days preaching hatred. For some it is financially profitable, and they have made careers out of spewing their hateful bile on various social-media platforms and in political and social commentary on TV. Despite their rhetoric being abhorrent, ignorant, and toxic, many social-media platforms continue to allow these individuals to continue with their hate, lies, and conspiracy theories with little or no pushback. They allow users to light the fuse of hatred and violence.

Social-media hate-mongers lump whole races, communities, and religions together, often posting offensive and fear-inducing content and misinformation. It was this kind of fear and hatred whipped up by such people that contributed to the 2016 murder of British politician Jo Cox. Jo was shot and stabbed multiple times in broad daylight while on the streets of Birstall in West Yorkshire. Her murderer, Thomas Mair, was a fifty-two-year-old local man who was obsessed with the Nazi Party and the far-right. He was an avid consumer of far-right content, having subscribed to various online hate groups that encourage such violence.

Hateful people often forget or don't even realise that the Universe is keeping score. At some point, we must account for our actions and pay our dues. No one is above the law of the Universe, and we need to be mindful of the consequences of attacking others and stoking the flames of hate.

Social media is a great example of a place where you can find millions of people preaching hatred and anger against all manner of things. Don't let their hatred steer you off course. You are the captain of your ship, and it is your hands on the wheel. This is your life and your responsibility.

Something which has helped me greatly as I continue my journey and work to becoming a better person is the following idea: how you choose to perceive, interpret, and react to events can mean the difference between moving forward in life or feeling stressed, angry, and dwelling on the past for years to come. I can choose to let someone else pull my emotional strings and, with that, control my happiness, or I can take control and refuse to be dragged down into negativity.

What I try to do these days is view past negative events as lessons learned. I choose to no longer be held a prisoner by my past. I can only learn the lessons from my past in the hope that I do not make the same mistakes again. As I witness the dangerous rhetoric, violence, and hate speech that is all too prevalent today, I have to hope that those doing it wake up to the reality of what they are doing. Imagine if they channelled all the energy they presently use spreading hate and anger into spreading love and kindness. Imagine a place like that. Now you move forward and be part of the solution, not the problem.

EMBRACE DISCOMFORT

When was the last time you seriously asked yourself what you want out of this life? It seems that this extremely important question (probably the most important question you can ask yourself) is often given very little thought. Most people are just going round on the hamster wheel of life, waiting for something to happen. To most, life is just a seemingly uncontrollable series of events which they must deal with as they occur. They believe they are completely powerless to direct and influence their lives. How many times have you heard people ask, "What can I do about it?" when faced with something they feel they have no control over? The answer to that question is simple: *everything*.

When I ask clients what they want out of this life, I often get the answer, "I don't know" or "I'm not sure." All of these people are adults who have had their entire lives to think about what it is they want from life, yet most have no idea. To settle for stumbling through life, dealing with whatever it throws at you, and having no plan seems like a wasted opportunity.

I truly believe most of us know what we want and desire out of this life. The issue, for many, is fear. We are afraid to admit what we want and thus challenge the excuse for continuing on the hamster wheel of comfort and familiarity. If this sounds like you, I invite you to do the following meditation exercise to reveal your deepest desires:

1. Find a quiet place and make yourself comfortable. This is your time, so turn off mobile phones and mute all distractions from the outside world for the next 20 minutes to half-hour.

2. Sit in silence and concentrate only on your breathing. Focus on the breath going in and the breath going out.

3. While focusing on your breathing, you may begin to have intrusive thoughts enter your mind. Some of them may well seem quite random, like the need to compile a mental shopping list, or ruminating on a conversation you had several days ago.

4. Catch those thoughts as they enter your mind and stop them in their tracks before they develop into bigger, even more complex and distracting thoughts. Once you have relaxed and stopped the intrusive thoughts, you will be able to hear your inner, authentic voice. What is it telling you? Let it be as extravagant as it wants. Nothing is out of bounds, and there are no limits and or judgements in this state of relaxation and deep thought.

5. Ask your inner, authentic self what your ideal life would look like. You already know what you want—it is there for you and always has been. What you have been doing most of your life is blocking out that inner voice, and

the real you. Don't be afraid to take this time, now, to truly recognise your dreams.

You have likely suppressed the dreamer within you because you are afraid and don't want to hear it speak the truth. You fear facing what you really want because you know that means change, hard work, and discomfort. You may also think that to pursue what you want would be selfish, and you aren't deserving of anything good.

I'm here to tell you that you are deserving of everything you desire. You are important. No one else on this earth is quite like you, and you are unique and beautiful. The world needs to see the greatness you possess that stays imprisoned inside yourself. Stop denying the world your greatness.

As humans, we are naturally averse to discomfort. We are programmed to view discomfort as a potential danger, a negative, and something to be avoided at all costs. But the truth is very different. Discomfort is where the growth is and where the treasure lies. If you want to build muscle, you must first stress the muscle, feeling discomfort by taking it into what is known as the "burn" through lifting weights. The burn is where the growth happens.

If you want to move on from whatever situation you presently find yourself in, you are going to have to get out of your comfort zone and embrace discomfort. I tell the students who come to my self-defence classes that one of the biggest battles they will ever have is in the mind. We need to silence the negative voices within our heads and not let it have dominance over us. We need to take risks and take a leap of faith into uncertainty, trusting that the Universe has our backs and will do everything it can to deliver what is best for us.

It is natural to crave certainty in life, but there really is no such thing. Not one of us can predict with certainty what will happen in the next hour, let alone in the next day, week, or year. We have no certainty in life other than the now.

If you did the above relaxation exercise and listened to your inner voice, hopefully you now have some idea what it is that you want to do with your life. Make it happen, stop procrastinating, and start now! The cemetery is full of broken dreams and people who, if given the chance to have another crack at this great adventure, would do things very differently than they did the first time around. Stop dreaming and truly live and experience all that this life has to offer before it's too late. Remember, it is you who is in the driving seat of life, and it is you who gets to steer in the direction you wish your life to go in.

You get one go at this. You have been blessed and given this gift, this chance, this fantastic opportunity to live a life. Don't waste the privilege.

POSITIVE VS. NEGATIVE MENTALITY

In my self-defence classes, I teach a concept called pre-emptive striking, which basically means, "Don't wait to be hit; hit first, and hit fucking hard." If you wait to be hit, you could be unconscious on the floor with your head being used as a football or a trampoline before you even realise you are in a fight. I also teach my students about the importance of mentality when facing a potentially violent person. If you tell yourself you are going to lose, get hurt, and that you can't handle what is happening, then that is probably the result you will get.

This applies to everything in life. What you tell yourself determines what will happen next. What you think about becomes reality.

When I find myself in a stressful or challenging situation, I have gotten into the habit of telling myself the following affirmations:

"I can handle this."
"This is not a problem."
"I am strong and fearless."

These are mantras that I repeat in my head to push out any self-defeating doubts and negativity. I replace doubt with positivity and a belief that, YES, I can handle this. I can handle anything that gets thrown my way. And the fact I am still here, despite a fair amount of shit being thrown my way over the years, is proof of this.

You wouldn't go into the boxing ring telling yourself you're going to lose. If you did, then you would almost certainly see yourself defeated. Any professional athlete will tell you that positivity is a massive part of how they approach competitions. They go in believing they *can* and *will* win. If they didn't, what would be the point in participating?

We have two inner voices, both of which are competing for our attention. Whichever you choose to listen to will determine much of your life. Let's name these two voices Mr. Negative and Mr. Positive (very original, I know).

Personally, Mr. Negative had almost complete control of my brain for many years. Whenever I had a positive thought, Mr. Negative would immediately pop up to cast a shadow of doubt over everything. My imagination would go into overdrive, and I would begin to imagine all manner of worst-case scenarios befalling me. These were all self-defeating messages. I would end up talking myself out of whatever plan I had and just stay rooted in the miserable place I was, feeling depressed, helpless and imprisoned.

There is a lot to be said about the old Latin proverb, "Fortune favours the brave," because it truly does. What we need to be is brave and tell Mr. Negative to shut the fuck up. We need to bring Mr. Positive to the forefront of our minds and allow positivity to be the dominant voice we hear. We need to believe in ourselves.

I want you to understand that you are far more powerful and stronger than you realise. You have the strength and ability to face up to any challenge and overcome it. Everything you need is already within you: strength, courage, determination—they are all there within, you need to stop suppressing them and let them rise to the surface.

To use another Latin phrase, "Carpe diem"—seize the day. Do the things you want to do today, because tomorrow is not guaranteed.

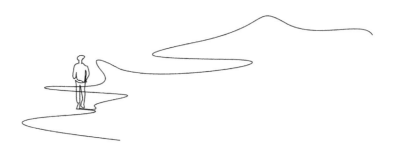

STRESS AND WORRY

Here is an unquestionable truth to remember: you have overcome every adversity and challenge you have faced in your life.

Just think about that fact for a minute, let it sink in. You are stronger than you think you are.

I am now in my fifties, and during my time on this rock hurtling through space I have faced numerous challenges—all of which seemed huge and insurmountable at the time. I have been so stressed over issues that I have literally made myself sick. Looking back, I can see in the main that they were all trivial matters.

I have lost countless nights of sleep over the years, lying awake in bed with endless thoughts going on in my mind. This still sometimes happens to me today. When it does, I now grab a pen and paper (which I always keep on my bedside table) and I write down a list of the thoughts going through my mind. I literally take the thoughts that are worrying me and keeping me awake out of my head and transfer them onto the paper. This helps to clear my mind. When I wake in the morning and read back what is written, it becomes clear that the worry and stress was needlessly exaggerated.

They say that with age comes wisdom, and in at least some aspects, that seems to be true for me. I have learned that worrying and stressing doesn't change a single thing. It won't make the situation go away and it certainly won't help the situation. All it will do is make you feel sick. Stress is a caustic substance which, if left unchecked, will swill around your internal organs and destroy you from within. Stress and worry are not your friends. You can see pain in the faces of those who have let stress and constant anguish dominate their lives. It is etched upon their worn-out faces, and they look old before their time.

I want you to think about a major challenge you have faced in your life and remember the stress and worry it caused you at the time. Remember the hours you spent with it dominating your thoughts. Remember the sickness that you felt in the pit of your stomach every time you thought about it, and the sleepless nights it caused. Now, ask yourself: did that stress and worry change anything about the outcome? The answer to that question is very likely *no*. All the worry, stress, and torment you put yourself through didn't change a single thing.

Next question: despite all of the worry and stress, did you eventually overcome and deal with whatever the issue was? The answer to that question is *yes, you did*. Otherwise, you wouldn't be here. You came out the other side and it is now behind you. All things shall pass—this is another unquestionable truth.

That doesn't mean that you should never worry. We are humans, and have a tendency to worry about our friends and family—and ourselves, at times. It is practically impossible to stop worrying altogether, but there can be proportionality. Worrying about if the supermarket will have what you want tomorrow is a pointless worry. Getting stressed in traffic is a pointless stress. Both of these things are beyond your control, and worrying will not change a single thing about the outcome.

Remember that you are the one who has control over how you react to things.

Life will always throw challenges at you—life is an ongoing series of events and challenges. Going into a meltdown each time you face a challenge will not help you in anyway.

The next time you are faced with something difficult, think, "I can handle this. I will deal with this. This shall pass." And repeat and repeat and repeat.

As I write this, I am facing a challenge of my own: I have a calf injury which is extremely painful when walking up stairs or any slope. I am having physiotherapy for the injury, and when I am back to fitness, I hope to visit the world's highest Irish bar located in the Himalayas, at the foot of Mount Everest. The pub is located in a village called Namche Bazaar. You cannot get there by motor vehicle, so the journey in itself is the adventure. It involves a rather perilous flight from Kathmandu to a small airport in a town called Lukla, where the runway is so short that only small planes can land there.(The runway is so short that it had to be made sloped to help slow the landing aircraft down.) Once the plane has committed to land, there is no turning back, as the runway is surrounded by mountains, making a turnaround of the approaching aircraft impossible. The flight is only the first part of the journey; it is followed by a two-day trek on foot through the mountains. I am not a walker; I haven't done a trek in my life. My feet tend to ache after just a few miles of walking on a normal surface, so goodness knows how I'm going to cope with a rocky, uneven surface going uphill, but do it I will. It is about challenging myself and enjoying the journey. While these travel plans are quite a scary prospect for someone like myself, I am committed to minimising my stress and worry before the event. I will instead focus on healing my injury and preparing for the trip as best I can, leaving my fears and anxiety about things outside of my control behind.

I'm told the scenery in Namche Bazaar is breathtaking, but the real reward once the journey is complete will be a pint in the pub.

NOBODY'S PUNCHBAG

I feel I must be truthful and confess that, whilst at my secondary school, I did partake in behaviour that can only be described as bullying. It is something I am deeply ashamed of and regret. I can only hope that my appalling behaviour did not go on to affect those I bullied too much in their later life. (If you are reading this and were someone I bullied, I send you my heartfelt apologies.)

I also found myself bullied in school.

When I was about ten or eleven years old, I was the victim of two bullies who lived down the road from me, and who I frequently had to pass on my way home from town or school. I was the victim of their unprovoked attacks on numerous occasions, and was in terror every time I had to pass where they hung out. I was petrified that they would be waiting for me, and that I would yet again be victim to their punches and kicks. As a child, I was in constant fear of attack. Whether it was from other kids or from the untrustworthy adults that my mother was constantly warning me about, I felt threatened all the time. It is fair to say that I wasn't a confident child.

But one day, while walking home and feeling the usual terror at the thought of bumping into my two tormentors, something snapped within me. I had had enough. No more.

I was tired of being their victim. Tired of being their punch bag. Tired of being held in terror.

I was just fucking tired of it all and I decided that today was the day I was going to fight back. I felt an anger within me and an inner voice proclaiming, "I'm not going to stand for it anymore: I'm not going to be bullied. I'm walking home and I'm going to be ready. If they show up, I'm going to fucking fight back. Fuck em. How dare they do this to me?"

This was the first time I ever remember saying to myself, *no more, this stops now*. I was no longer going to be bullied, scared, or filled with fear. I was fucking ready.

As I approached the area where my two tormentors were usually to be found, the familiar stomach churning and fear began to take over my body and mind. I now know this to be the effects of adrenaline entering my body. I was literally in fight or flight mode. But that day, there would be no flight—only fight.

I neared a little side street on my route and I had a feeling inside that they would appear. Sure enough, there they were, and they saw me. One of them was on a bike, eating a sandwich, and the other on foot. I saw them smile at each other at the thought of the fun they were about to have using me as their human punch bag again.

But today, instead of turning and running away, I carried on walking towards them. As I got nearer, nothing happened; they just continued to watch me. As I got right up to them, nothing happened, and I just walked past them... then after I had walked a few more yards away from them I felt a smack on the back of my head. I put my hand to where I had been hit and felt the greasy butter from the sandwich which the one on the bike had just smashed into the back of my head. His blond-haired mate then walked up to me and began to speak. I knew this was his normal buildup before the physical attack. "Fuck you, Blondie," I thought as I threw a punch that hit him on the side of his head—just the one punch, but that was enough to stop him in his tracks and prevent his planned attack. He covered up his face, crouched down, and cowered. Before today it was always him that had done the hitting, and he sure as hell didn't like being the one to get hit. His friend on the bike, now a few yards away and watching, decided after witnessing his friend get hit that he wasn't feeling so brave. He began to ride away. The fucking coward didn't even have the guts to face me.

I remember thinking to myself that this had been too fucking easy. One punch had reduced Blondie into a cowering heap, and Biker Boy had also suddenly been hit by cowardice and was riding off as fast as he could. Pumped full of adrenaline and eager to exact revenge on both of the bullies, I began to chase him. I shouted for him to stop, get off his bike, and fight, but he was too fast. I saw him look behind a few times to make sure I wasn't catching up. I called after him, letting him know that the next time I saw him it will be him getting punched.

For the first time ever, I had faced my bullies, and it felt fucking fantastic. Not only had I faced them head on, I had beaten them. They were indeed cowards, and they had crumbled as soon as I had fought back. Everything I had been told as a child about bullies was confirmed as true.

I was never bothered by the characters in question ever again. All my walks home after that day were unchallenged. The two tormentors who had made my walks home full of terror were now history.

As children we are told bullies are really cowards, and the best way to deal with them is to face up to them and fight back. This in my experience is absolutely true, although I accept it can be a daunting and scary thing to do.

In adult life, the bullying may not be physical. It may manifest itself as constant criticism or personal abuse; whichever it is, the approach should still be the same—confront the perpetrator and let them know you will not tolerate it. I have found in circumstances such as this that confronting a bully with the truth and facts is enough to defeat them. It sends a very clear message to them that you are not their punch bag, you won't just sit back and let them do what they are doing, you will confront and you will fight back.

Bullies only ever pick on those they perceive to be weaker than themselves; they pick on people who they believe they can dominate and will not fight back. The moment you fight back, their power has gone. So if you are presently the victim of bullying I want you to be angry, because you should be angry. I want you to be brave, and I want you to stand up for yourself and fight back, because you are worth it; you are worth fighting for.

Draw your line in the sand. That line is where you will not allow anyone to cross, and if someone should try to cross that line, then the gloves are off, and you will defend yourself. Know your worth, know your value, know what you are prepared to fight for—and I don't just mean in the physical sense. If you don't know what you are prepared to defend and fight for, then how will you know when the line has been crossed? When I work with people for the first time on a one-to-one basis, most have never even thought about what their values are, or what they are prepared to defend. So I urge you now to sit down and give this some thought. Because until you know the answers to those important questions, you will not know where your line is, let alone when it has been crossed.

Personally I am very clear in my mind what I am prepared to defend. I am very clear where my line in the sand is, and if anyone should begin to come near that line, I will if possible give a warning. If the line is crossed, then I will defend what I value with everything I have got. I know my worth, and I know my value. Not in a conceited, I-love-myself way, but in the sense of my value to others whom I love dearly. We all have people who love us and for whom we are important. In my case it is my girls, and I am too important to them to allow someone to bully or potentially hurt me.

TREAT OTHERS AS YOU WISH
TO BE TREATED

The other day, my twenty-one-year-old daughter rang me to tell me about a message she had received from her boss. My daughter is a good worker, always on time, and always works her hardest. She is extremely good at what she does. Her boss, on the other hand, is a bully—pure and simple. No matter what my daughter does, it isn't good enough. She is constantly criticised, passed over for treats and bonuses while other employees receive them right in front of her, and subjected to her boss's awful, unwarranted behaviour.

Her boss has a history of behaving in this way. She has bullied countless now ex-employees, and in the less than two years that my daughter has been working at her establishment, a number of very talented and hardworking people have left, all citing the boss's intolerable behaviour.

Sadly, these kinds of deliberate actions upset my daughter and made her feel rubbish about herself. I explained to her that this is no reflection on her, but rather a reflection on the sort of person her boss is. We discussed an exit strategy where she can get everything she needs from the job—experience and a qualification—and also see the light at the end of the tunnel. Once she has her qualification in about three months' time, she will be gone. In the meantime, she is getting the experience she needs and has also begun to develop a website and plan for her own business. Using her current job for her benefit and maintaining a mindset of being in control, she will have great joy in walking out the door and dropping her boss right in the shit in the process.

In the early days of my working career, a union rep once told me that business owners should invest in and treat their workers with respect. His theory was quite simple: treat people as you wish to be treated yourself. Show them respect and kindness and you will get the same in return. As most of us know, and as my daughter has recently learned, this isn't always the way it goes.

In my working life, I've had bosses I wouldn't piss on if they were on fire, because they treated me like shit. The only reason I worked for them was for the money. I went through the motions, but there was no pride in my work and I never gave my best. I felt no motivation to go an extra inch, let alone a mile. I've also had bosses who treated me with respect, paid me fairly, and actually cared for their employees. For those people, I would go that extra mile.

I once worked in a large distribution centre for a major UK supermarket chain. The job was a soul-destroying affair, paying the minimum wage and requiring me to pick food orders and pack them in metal cages for distribution to various stores around the country.

The supervisors were paid a small amount of extra money on top of the minimum wage to do the dirty work of the well-paid managers. A lot of the supervisors really thought they had made it and seemed to have forgotten where they came from. With their clipboards in hand, they would strut around like some kind of appointed gods. In truth, they were just poorly paid cannon fodder like the rest of us. But for many, that little bit of power went to their heads and made them bullies.

Like kings, they would stride around the little areas of the warehouse for which they were responsible. These sad, pathetic bastards, who had once been just order pickers like the rest of us, traded in the camaraderie and friendship of their fellow order pickers to gain a few extra pounds a week and the privilege of sitting on the canteen table with the other sad bastard supervisors. In the main, they were detested and despised by everyone, even the higher management.

Some of the supervisors seemed to thrive on talking down to people and ordering them around like they were drill sergeants on the parade ground. The arrogance and attitude of some of them made me want to smash them hard in the face several times. (I was operating at a very low frequency back then.) I imagined screaming into their bloodied faces, "Don't ever fucking talk to me in that way again." (Again, this was a time when I could be prone to let my fists do the talking—not something I would advocate at all these days.)

During my short period working at the distribution centre, I had one supervisor—some jumped-up little skid-mark who was ten years my junior—ask me what my ambition was within the company. He asked me if I would like to become a supervisor too, and preside, like him, over a picking line. Or maybe, if I played my cards right and kept my head down, become a forklift driver unloading and loading lorries? I thought to myself, "What, and be a fucking wanker like you? No thanks, mate, I'd sooner stick hot pins in my scrotum than end up like you."

This made me realise that the job had given me all I could take from it, and it was time to move on. So just as I would advise my daughter years later, I developed an exit strategy. After a couple of months of working there, which had got me through the Christmas season, I decided my time was up. I planned to walk out at the next sarcastic word from one of the supervisors.

Judgement day came shortly after, when I was put onto the meat line, despite being a vegetarian and my bosses knowing this would offend me. I knew this was to be the day. I told no one and proceeded to look as though I was working normally. I was given my papers with details of the orders I was to pick for the various stores. I then proceeded to completely disregard what was on the order sheets and just picked what I wanted to pick, in whatever quantity I wanted to pick, and distributed this across the UK stores.

I spent a couple of hours doing this, completely fucking up every store order I could and smiling to myself, imagining the absolute chaos for the stores when they got the deliveries and found themselves short or overstocked. I also knew, more importantly, that this would result in angry store managers from around the UK ringing up the distribution centre in a panic. And best of all—the supervisors would bear the brunt of the backlash.

When the morning tea break came around, I calmly walked out of the centre and drove home with a massive smile on my face, pleased with my morning's work and knowing that the centre was now a man down and would be looking for me.

All this could have been avoided had I been treated and spoken to with respect instead of being looked down upon and spoken to like I was a piece of dirt.

We are all humans, who are loved and important to someone. No one would like to think of their loved ones being spoken to and treated like dirt, so be mindful how you speak to others. Always treat people with respect no matter who they are, or who you are. From the CEO to the person who cleans the toilets, everyone matters and deserves respect.

Without my daughter and people like her, her boss would have no business. When my daughter leaves, her business will be losing an extremely hard-working and conscientious employee, and all because of the way her boss has behaved.

CONFRONTING MORTALITY

We have one life with which we are gifted. If we are lucky, we may get between seventy and eighty years. If we are really lucky, we may get a little longer. But in the great scheme of time on earth, our lives amount to a mere flicker of an eye.

When you die, your life will be summarised by the dash between the date you were born and the date you died—the whole of your existence on earth will be represented by that one line. What do you want that line to represent?

There is nothing like a crisis to get us moving. A crisis can help us realise that we are after all mortal, and death is one day inevitable. But that's only because we were lucky enough to be alive. A crisis can have us re-evaluating our lives, looking at what is important and what is not, asking ourselves what it is that we want to get out of our lives. What legacy do we want to leave behind?

For some, a health scare and finding themselves potentially staring death in the face will kick-start that evaluation. Many will feel there is still unfinished business, lots of things they want to do, and that they are not yet ready to leave this planet. They will promise themselves that, if they get through the crisis and survive, they will start to live life to its fullest. Perhaps they will write the book they've been thinking about writing for years. Or go on that adventure, buy that dream car, book to go on that world cruise, etc. Suddenly finding themselves facing their own mortality and the realisation that life does end, they will finally start living.

When we are young, we think time is infinite. We think we have forever and we don't realise that, with every passing day, our balance of allotted time on the earth becomes smaller. Then one day, we wake up and wonder where all that time has gone. The realisation that we don't have forever hits us with a jolt.

The realisation that my own time on this planet was not actually infinite hit me as I approached my fortieth birthday. I became aware that I was probably getting towards the halfway stage of my life, and soon I would have more days behind me than were left in front of me. None of us know how long we will be given on this earth. In fact, the only certainty we have is that with each passing day, we get ever closer to the grave. Of course, this is unpleasant to think about, but our clock continues ticking down and our time diminishes anyway. How most of us cope with this fact is by putting it to the back of our minds and doing our best to forget about our impending doom. Every now and then, however, something occurs which makes us think about our inevitable demise, and we start to evaluate our lives. For some, this can be completely life-changing; for others, it's no more than a fleeting thought, soon forgotten.

Death is the one thing that unites us all: the rich and powerful, the poor and downtrodden. Power and money cannot buy immortality; only a more comfortable time spent on this planet. One day, even the seemingly powerful will be returned to the earth, no different from everyone else.

When considering their mortality, many people will write a

bucket list of things they'd like to achieve before they die. But why does it take something drastic to happen for us to wake up and realise how fortunate we are to have been given this chance of life, and to start actually living the life we dreamed of? Wouldn't it be so much better to be living our best lives now?

I often hear people say things such as, "Once the kids are grown up, we will go travelling." I know that I have been guilty of using my children as an excuse for not living life to the fullest. We always make excuses for why we are not pursuing our dreams now. We promise that one day, in the future, we will pursue our dreams. But deep inside, we know that we are lying to ourselves. We project into the future to keep today tolerable, believing that all we have to do is get through the dramas and trauma of today—tomorrow will be better. But tomorrow is not guaranteed.

I want to get you questioning your life's purpose. Don't settle for taking whatever shit gets thrown your way and accepting it because, well, that's just the way it is, isn't it? Don't accept that life just sucks and it's always been that way. NO! NO! FUCKING NO! I want you to be brave and be the change. Prove to yourself and others that, YES, you can do whatever you want. This is your life you are living and you are responsible for it and how it is lived. Dear reader, it's time for you to "get in the game," as our American friends would say.

As an adult in charge of your own life and destiny, you don't have to wait for permission to pursue whatever it is you want to pursue. (But if you are wanting permission, then let me be the one to grant it to you right now.) No one owns you; you are an independent, living being. Go and push the boundaries of your own self-imposed limitations. Dip your toe into the waters you once felt were off limits to you and take comfort in knowing that the Universe has your back.

Sometimes, we just need to take that leap of faith to break free from whatever shackles confine and limit us. Don't wait for a crisis to realise that your life is meaningful and important.

FROM DOUBT TO MOTIVATION

Many of us have a desire to be brave and break out from the mundane. We have a deep wish to make our lives somehow meaningful and to be someone that others may look up to—or even envy. We have moments where we feel anything is possible, and we have fantastic ideas and dreams where we plan to do incredible things. Some of us may even start to formulate a plan of action to achieve those things. But then, negative voices enter our head and begin asking questions and sowing the seeds of doubt in our minds. *What if it goes wrong? I will look stupid and people will laugh. It's too hard. I will fail, I always fail. I shouldn't get above my station in life.*

I'm sure you are familiar with such negative thoughts. Some of the greatest minds, artists, writers, poets, actors, and musicians have come from similar backgrounds of doubt, but they did not allow the negativity from others around them drag them down and make them stop believing.

For example, take the world's most successful band of all time: The Beatles. They were four working-class lads from Liverpool who had a dream to become a famous band and play concerts around the world. They refused to let knockbacks set them off course from their desire to make it in the music industry. John Lennon's aunt, Mimi, brought him up from a young child and famously said to John, "The guitar is alright as a hobby, John, but you'll never make a living at it." When he became famous, he had those words engraved on a plaque and sent it to her at the house he had bought her in Sandbanks.

On January 1st 1962, The Beatles recorded an audition tape at the London recording studios of Decca Records, hoping to get a record deal with them. Decca rejected The Beatles. The Decca executives are famously quoted as saying, "Guitar groups are on the way out," and "The Beatles have no future in show business."

Had The Beatles listened to others and given up at the first hurdle, we would never have had the great music they went on to produce. We must be stubbornly determined and believe in ourselves. Guard against those who criticise, and chase out negative thoughts from your mind.

When we become parents, we often forget about our own needs. We can end up feeling guilt when we have done something for ourselves, believing that we are being selfish or extravagant to even consider pursuing something for ourselves. This really is not the case, despite what others may say. You are important, and should not lose sight of your own importance as a human who has desires and needs. These do not stop the moment you become a parent, and you should not feel guilty for having them. Having children should not mean you have to stop living your own life, and it doesn't mean you have to stop pursuing your own dreams. What being a parent does require you to do is find a way to still have those adventures without putting everyone and everything you care about at risk.

Your time on earth goes extremely quickly. One minute you are in your twenties, and next thing you know, you are in your fifties.

Ex-Beatle George Harrison, shortly before his death, reflected on this in an interview: "It doesn't take long from being seventeen to being fifty-seven, forty years just goes like that."

One day you will look in the mirror and the reality of how quickly those years have passed will hit you. The face staring back at you is no longer the face you have in your mind's eye. It isn't the face of your youth, when you had forever and everything still seemed possible. The face is worn and tired; it has lines where the skin was once smooth and soft; the eyes aren't as bright and as wide as they once were; the skin no longer glows; the body is no longer as toned. You wonder how this happened, and realise that, while your mind has remained steadfast, your body has aged.

Imagine this scenario: you began a job you despise many years ago, and promised yourself that you would give it only a year at the most. You'd get some money saved up and then go on an adventure or go for your dream job. The year passed by, and in that time you bought a car and decided now wasn't the right time to jack the job in. You promise yourself just one more year, and then you will be gone.

Then you meet someone. You fall in love and begin to talk of marriage, so you tell yourself, "I'll just give it another year to help pay for the wedding and then I'll leave." Next up is a mortgage that keeps you mentally shackled in the job you hate. Then it's kids and, before you know it, a decade has gone by in the job you now hate more than anything else, and which you had promised yourself was just a stopgap before you pursued your dreams.

Does this scenario ring any bells with you? It certainly does with me. I used all of the excuses above for staying in a job I hated, and it actually made me so ill and caused me so much stress that I had to take a year off sick after coming close to a total nervous breakdown.

Readers, I am here to tell you that now is the right time to break out and go for it. Don't ask yourself, "What's the worst that can happen?" Instead, ask, "What's the best that can happen?" Think of all those possibilities and great things just waiting around the corner; it's there waiting for you. So start to take the action you need, to achieve what you desire.

You make your own good fortune and you attract what you think about and pursue. If I sit at home all day and do nothing but watch TV, I'm going to attract very little into my life. However, if I get out there in the world and start doing the right work, connecting to the right people, and visiting the right places which bring me closer to those things I desire, then it will begin to happen. Surround yourself with people and things that motivate you. Remember, as the saying goes, *you are the company that you keep*. Being in the right company puts you in the frequency for that which you desire. If you want to be a writer then start to seek out the company of other writers. If you want to be a plumber, then seek out other plumbers. It is that simple, but vital.

Being suddenly plunged into a crisis will motivate you to get off your arse and do the work, but don't wait for a crisis to be pushed into positive action. Start taking positive action now. You already have the spark within you; it has always been there, but dormant because you have been coasting. Make a plan, write down where you want to be in a year's time, and then map out how you plan to get there. Start now and stop making excuses. Alternatively stay exactly where you are right now. The choice is yours and yours alone.

NO GOOD COMES FROM VIOLENCE

It is fair to say that violence has been something of a theme throughout my life. In my youth, I was attracted to the violence at football games. As a young child, it was exciting to watch the older lads fighting outside or inside the football ground of Elland Road, home to my beloved Leeds United. As I got older and into my teens, I also began to get involved in football violence. At first, it was just on the periphery of skirmishes, but it soon escalated into full-blown fights with opposition supporters.

In the 1980s, Leeds fans were notorious for trouble, and unquestionably amongst the most violent and feared fans in the country. They had a huge following that would travel the length and breadth of the country to support the team. A large number of those who travelled to away matches were like me: looking for trouble.

I soon found myself making friends with other like-minded Leeds fans from around the UK, who like me all loved the buzz you got from fighting other teams' supporters.

The Leeds hooligans had become known as The Leeds United Service Crew. This was because they would travel on the normal service trains instead of the football special trains laid on by

British Rail. The fans who travelled by the football specials would be policed on the trains, and upon arrival at their destination, they would be met by large numbers of police on foot, horseback, and in vans, and then escorted to the football ground. By travelling on the normal service trains, we evaded the attention of the police and were free to hit the city centre and seek out opposition supporters.

Following Leeds United around the country was an obsession for me. The Service Crew and the mates I made were at that time like a family to me. It didn't matter what you did for a living or where you came from. On Saturday, we were as one. We were all equal. We were all Leeds and we had each other's backs. I imagine that it is probably the nearest you could get to the camaraderie of the armed forces.

The buzz, tension, and anticipation were immense when we were drinking in the opposition pubs in yet another city centre. It felt powerful and I felt like I belonged to something. We felt we were feared, and it was a very seductive and toxic mix. I was involved in the football hooligan scene on and off for a couple of decades. I found myself arrested on a number of occasions, and made appearances in court for football-related incidents.

Unless you have been a part of anything like this, it will most probably be hard for you to understand the emotions and feelings I have described. Many of you reading this will no doubt think people who indulge in football violence are scum and of low intelligence. This is not the case. I had a respectable day job, and I knew people from all walks of life who would be involved with the violence. I even knew of police officers who, on occasion, were involved in trouble.

The group of lads I hung around with became known to the Leeds United police spotters and we would be closely monitored by them whenever we arrived in a city centre. We were actually on first-name terms with the West Yorkshire police spotters, who travelled around the country keeping an eye on the Leeds United supporters and advising local police on any known faces. They would often pull us to one side and warn us that we were being watched by the local police who knew who we were and we would be advised to keep our heads down. There was almost a mutual respect between us and some of the spotters, it was like a game between us, they had a job to do which was prevent us from getting into any fights with opposition supporters, and we would try to evade detection. On one occasion at Tottenham away, Leeds were being badly beaten on the pitch, so about 15 minutes before full time, me and a mate decided we would leave early and get the tube back to the train station. As we left the ground we were quickly picked up by the local police who prevented us from going any further and detained us. We were escorted to an area where two police vans had been parked against a wall and we were placed in the space between the two vans, it was essentially a makeshift holding cell, in front of the vans was a line of police officers preventing us from leaving.

We were joined by about another twenty Leeds fans who had also been detained after trying to leave the game early. When the final whistle went fans began to leave the ground and make their way home, however those of us detained were not allowed to leave. One of the Leeds United spotters who we knew well came over to us and said they know who you are and are waiting until the area is clear and then they will let you go. So we waited until the area had mostly cleared, then the local police said "Right on your way lads" and walked off leaving us to make our way back to the tube station unescorted. We had only walked about twenty yards when all hell broke loose as a large group of Tottenham fans who had obviously been watching us from a distance saw their chance to attack, bottles and glasses started to rain down on us and we were heavily outnumbered; the shout of "stick together Leeds" rang out as we started to try fight our way through the group which was now surrounding us. Fists and kicks were flying in from all directions and I was starting to think, *this isn't going too well and we are going to get an absolute beating here.* Suddenly some mounted police appeared out of nowhere followed by other officers on foot, and the Tottenham started to scatter. We were now surrounded by police and amongst this sea of officers we saw our friendly Leeds United spotter who was clearly not happy at what the Metropolitan Police had done by letting us go unescorted. He began shouting at the local police "get some fucking vans here now and get these lads in them". Once the vans arrived we were bundled into them and driven to the tube station with the thud of missiles hitting them as we were driven off at speed. I saw the West Yorkshire police spotter in question the following week, and he expressed his anger at what had happened explaining he had been trying to get us released straight after the final whistle, but the local police wouldn't allow it. He then went on to say something which I always remember, "You might be a set of bastards Steve, but no one does that to my lads" he then smiled and said " You owe me one, so behave yourself today".

In 1995, I found myself kicked out of the local Leeds United supporters' club branch after I was arrested outside Wembley for attacking a group of opposition supporters, who in fairness to myself had thrown a full can of beer at me. At this time, I was completely immersed in the world of football hooliganism and I had also become a father to a beautiful baby girl. During the week, I had an extremely responsible job as a social worker, and yet there I was, actively looking for trouble at weekends. Towards the end of the 90s, I began to see the futility of it all. Although I was still going to games, I began to distance myself away from the violence and from some of my mates and acquaintances.

I would no longer hang around outside the ground after games looking for trouble. I began to feel sickened by the behaviour and views of some of my fellow supporters.

The final straw for me was getting arrested during an away game at Chelsea on May 15th, 2004, in what turned out to be Leeds United's last game in the Premier League for sixteen years. Without going into all the details, I was actually innocent. I was simply in the wrong place at the wrong time, and because I was someone who was known, I was dragged out from a large group of Leeds fans by riot police, thrown to the ground, given a good beating, handcuffed, and thrown into the back of a police van. I was then taken to a police station and locked up in a cell for a few hours. I was eventually released on bail, pending further enquiries, and although I had genuinely done nothing and was already stepping back from the hooligan scene, this arrest was a wakeup call. Thankfully, a few weeks later, all potential charges were dropped after police reviewed the video evidence and informed me I had no case to answer. The police officer in charge of reviewing my case used the phrase, "In the wrong place at the wrong time." Upon hearing this news, I breathed a huge sigh of relief and vowed that was it for me with football. Over the next couple of years, I completely left the world of hooliganism.

Once I removed myself from the culture, I realised just how pointless football violence is. I understand the buzz you can get from taking over a pub in some other team's city. I understand the camaraderie you feel when you are with others who all support the same team and are also prepared to fight for the same ridiculous cause you are. It is very seductive and addictive, especially for young men. But a far-right element has increasingly seeped its way in amongst many football firms, and racism and misogyny is rife. For someone like myself, who comes from the political left, it was always a hard thing to be around. This further endorsed my decision to remove myself from those circles.

To be involved in football hooliganism today is, frankly, a mug's game. CCTV is everywhere, and on top of that you have people recording footage on their mobile phones and uploading it to social media. Even if you don't get caught on the day of the trouble, that footage ensures that you will most likely be getting an early-morning call to your home from the police in the following weeks.

A football acquaintance of mine was arrested and charged several months after the violence he was involved in had been caught on video outside Elland Road. He was eventually tracked down and had to suffer the shame and humiliation of being arrested at home, in front of his family and neighbours. Was it really worth those few minutes of adrenaline he got from trading really crap punches (I saw the video) with opposition supporters? Was it worth the very real prospect of losing his liberty and the personal consequences which go with that, not to mention the stress and worry I know he went through along with his family prior to his court appearance? In the end, he was given a suspended prison sentence, along with a hefty fine and a football banning order. (The punishments given to football fans involved in any incident are similar. Anyone found guilty of a football-related offence these days faces being banned, having to report to police stations during games, or even having to hand in their passport during international games.)

I now look at this from the outside and I find it embarrassing and rather sad. Grown men with families, still behaving like they did in their teens, putting everything they have at risk for the sake of a punch-up at football.

So, what lessons have I learned from my violent past?

Firstly, no good ever comes from violence. Violence just returns more violence. Having a fight is the easy part of any confrontation as it is generally over within seconds, but the aftermath can last months, especially if the police are involved. You have to deal with all the stress and worry that accompanies any police involvement and charges you are facing. It is mentally exhausting, as your mind plays back the incident over and over again. You also have to deal with the fear and worry of a possible payback from friends and family of the person with whom you fought. You may even receive threatening texts, phone calls, or social-media messages vowing revenge. People could turn up at your home to threaten you and those you love with reprisals.

Trust me, when this happens, it plunges you into a very dark place. You feel physically sick with fear of the unknown; you struggle to get any sleep as you lie awake at night worrying and imagining the most horrific repercussions. When you walk out of your door, you are on hyper alert for a possible revenge attack. Every time your phone rings or announces a text, your heart beats fast and you have a feeling of dread. And each time this happens, you are left feeling completely drained afterwards.

My last serious physical fight happened about twenty years ago. The incident took place in a city centre, in broad daylight, on a Saturday afternoon, with lots of witnesses around. I had been drinking with my Leeds-supporting mates, and after we left one pub to make our way to another across town, one of the lads I was with (who could quite frankly start a fight on his own in an empty room), got into an argument with another group nearby.

I wasn't initially aware of what was going on until one of the lads in my group was confronted by two lads from the other group, one of whom had something in his hand which I could tell was soon going to be used as a weapon against my mate's head. Seeing this, I decided to intervene and hit the lad in question with a hard right cross before he could smash my mate's head in with whatever he was holding. My punch hit him right in the centre of his face, causing some collateral damage to his mouth and also hurting my fist in the process. (I should have hit him on the jaw line) The punch rocked him backwards and he held his face. His mate backed off as I screamed the question, "Do you fucking want some as well?" The lad I had hit then began to shout all kinds of threats from a few yards away, so I took a few steps towards him until he backed off further. After a few more words, he and his mate decided they didn't fancy anymore so they cleared off.

Meanwhile, the lad from my group who had started all of this had also been in a scuffle. Words were shouted between our two groups, but the other group backed away and we continued our way to the next pub. I thought nothing more of it.

The next day, there was news of a fight involving two groups in the city centre (where our fight had occurred), and police were looking for those involved. I rang up my mate, who I had saved from getting hit across the head, and we were both convinced it was us that the police were looking for and that it was only a matter of time before we were identified from CCTV footage and arrested. The lad I had hit during the fight was black, and although me hitting him had absolutely nothing to do with the colour of his skin, I was worried it would end up being seen as a racially motivated attack. This could mean a prison sentence, plus being portrayed as a racist by the media—something I definitely am not. For the next few days, I was sick with worry and nerves, expecting at any point a knock on the door from the police. Thankfully, the knock never came, and we learned that the police were investigating another group and not us.

I cannot explain the relief I felt when I heard this news. I had suffered days of anxiety which had made me feel sick, and I had convinced myself that me and my mate would end up in prison, resulting in dire consequences for my whole family. My daughters at the time of the incident were both young. Should I end up in prison, who would pay the mortgage? The reality was that the mortgage wouldn't be paid and my family would lose their home. My girls would be distraught at their dad going to prison and my wife would end up divorcing me. Over those few days following the incident, I had envisaged my whole world falling apart. I remember praying to God and asking to be given another chance, promising that I wouldn't have another violent confrontation ever again, unless it was to protect my life or my family.

This is the reality of the aftermath of violence, it is not like the violence glamorised by films and TV, which never show the actual consequences. They don't show you the sleepless nights worrying about possibly going to prison and losing everything you cherish.

As I have already stated, the actual fight is the easiest part. If a street fight lasts more than ten seconds, then it is considered a long fight. The respected UK martial artist Geoff Thompson talked of three-second fighting, because that is the average length of time a street fight lasts. The aftermath is the hardest part. The constant worry that means you can barely eat, the toxic effect that stress has on you internally, and the weakening of your immune system, causing illness, should have you asking yourself whether it is all worth it.

My conclusion, having lived that life, is a resounding *no*.

I am now incredibly ashamed of how I used to behave. Underneath all the bravado, noise, and violence was a very fragile, insecure, and frightened person with some massive ego issues.

If you foolishly choose to go down the road of violence, then be prepared to suffer stress, worry, and sleepless nights. Be prepared to suffer ill health brought on by the unrelenting stress of the situation, which you have created. And be prepared ultimately to lose your family and everything you hold dear, due to the fact you are serving a lengthy prison sentence.

A blank hard-drive

Trouble brewing aged 10

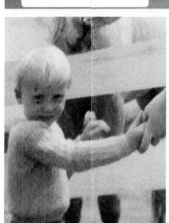

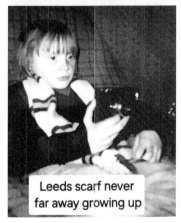

Leeds scarf never
far away growing up

Scooter run early 1980s

Somewhere in Europe
following England 1980s

Recording session
Drive Studios

Lansdown Grove Hotel
Bath 1989

LA 1989

Returning to combat sports
early 2000s

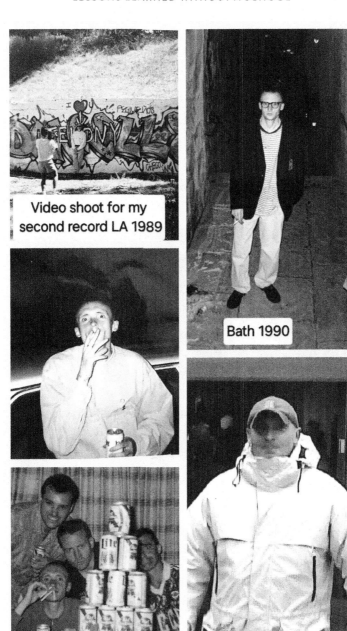

Video shoot for my second record LA 1989

Bath 1990

Another drunken LA night early 90s

Watching Leeds away late 90s

Today I'm on a more peaceful journey. At my happiest training, teaching or hanging out with my girls.

MATERIALISM

American author Chuck Palahniuk wrote, "We buy things we don't need, with money we don't have, to impress people we don't like."

One of many things I have learned in my five decades on this planet is that material wealth doesn't bring you happiness. Material possessions actually weigh you down. John Lennon speaks to this with the phrase, "When your prize possessions start to weigh you down," in The Beatles' song, "And Your Bird Can Sing." Material goods are nice to have, but they won't bring you true happiness. When you begin to break everything down and determine what is truly important, you will find that possessions are of little real value. Yet we get sucked into a system that puts so much value and worth on material possessions.

Businesses peddle you the fantasy that if you buy this product, you will be happy. They try to convince you that you really need the latest sixty-inch flat-screen TV, because the fifty-inch TV you currently have just isn't good enough anymore. With technology being so fast-moving these days, the latest model of the mobile phone you just spent hundreds of pounds on will literally be out of date within a few months. Advertisers bombard you with the message that you need bigger, better, *more.*

So, what can you do? You continue to work in the job that you hate, just so you can afford the latest up-to-date gizmo that you don't need in the fucking first place. We've been brainwashed by advertisers into believing that we need to buy products to be happy. This is how consumerism works. It sucks you in and, before you know it, you are a slave to the whole system; just feeding the relentless machine and keeping the whole merry-go-round going.

Now, I'm not going to tell you to stop consuming and drop out of society—that is not my message here. What you choose to do with your money and your life is completely up to you... but I want to make you aware of the system as I see it. You are, of course, free to disagree if you so wish (although this is really just a basic explanation of consumerism).

I have a number of personal stories regarding how I have fallen victim to consumerism myself, but for the purposes of this book, I will pick just one as an example.

In 2017, I bought myself a car—a Jaguar XF. It had pretty much everything I wanted: luxury heated and cooled seats, a leather interior, satnav, bluetooth—all the luxuries you would expect from Jaguar. It was the first time I had ever bought a truly luxurious car and I loved it. It never let me down once. I had this car for several years and had put a few miles on the clock, but it was still in great condition and drove beautifully. But I decided I wanted a new Jaguar. I started to look online and found one with less mileage. It was also four years newer and had a few extra gadgets. I convinced myself that owning this car would make me extremely happy. So, I went out and bought it, and for the first few days, I was a very happy man. But after a couple of weeks, it became just another car; a means of getting myself from A to B. I didn't even think about the fact I was driving a luxury Jaguar anymore. The initial happiness and joy from buying the car soon disappeared, and I was back to my normal unhappy state of being at that time.

The best material goods can ever do is mask your real state of mind for a short period of time. A lot of deeply unhappy people look for their next purchase fix to temporarily lessen the underlying feeling of misery and depression. Consumerism and the buying of material items will not fix whatever is truly going on within. I have met many extremely wealthy people over the years in my line of work, and I can tell you that many of them are extremely unhappy, despite appearing to have it all on a material level. They suffer from high stress levels and are worried to the point that it makes them physically ill. Many suffer from paranoia, believing that people are after their money, or that their employees are trying to screw them over in some way.

I have met people who are fantastically wealthy and can buy anything they want, yet they are deeply unhappy inside and have openly told me so when I have spoken with them.

With wealth comes responsibility, especially if you are employing people, and with that comes immense stress. I had one wealthy client tell me he regrets not being there for his kids when they were growing up. He told me he was always too busy building up his very successful business empire; so busy that he never really saw his kids when they were growing up. Sure, he sent them to the best private schools in his area, and they had horses and went on fantastic holidays. But even on holiday, he was working.

As I sat in his office and listened to this unhappy man, now in his early seventies, tell me he wished he had taken time out of work to enjoy his kids, I actually felt sorry for him. Here he was, looking back on his life and on what to the outside world appeared to be a hugely successful career. His kids had grown up and left home, and it was now just him and his wife. He had a beautiful house and a top-of-the-range Mercedes sitting on the drive, but he would have traded all of that in to have those years back when his children were young, and for the chance to be truly present in their lives.

I'm not saying that you shouldn't work hard, if that's what you want, but it is important to get the balance right. Don't sacrifice all those precious moments in your family life. Be present, because you will never get those moments back, no matter how rich you are. I am reminded of this famous quote by Oscar Wilde: "No man is rich enough to buy back his past."

Thinking back, I realise now that one of the happiest times of my life was when I had the least in terms of money and material wealth. In 1989-90, I had no car, very little in the form of savings, and was employed in a poorly paid porter's job at a hotel in Bath. I showed residents up to their hotel rooms as I carried their cases, and I also laid on enough charm to earn some decent tips during my shifts, which were enough to pay for my nights out. I was having the best time of my life in many ways, and working with a great bunch of young people, all in a similar position to me. Many were living away from home for the first time, so it was an exciting time for all of us. We played at being grown ups, responsible for ourselves, for the first time.

We would all go out together to the various pubs and clubs of Bath. I was living pretty much hand-to-mouth, but I didn't care or worry. I had fallen truly in love for the first time in my life, and it had quickly made me realise that what I had thought was love previously was nothing like the overwhelming, deep, and true love I was experiencing then. Despite having very few possessions, I was having a great time. I was free and I was in love; nothing was weighing me down. The world was, as they say, there at my feet.

In the Bible, Luke 12:15 says, "Be on your guard against all kinds of greed; a man's life does not consist in the abundance of his possessions."

For me, my unhappiness grew bigger as I began to gain more material goods—to the point that they completely filled a large, four-bed detached house, including the loft, which was crammed full of things I no longer needed but hadn't thrown away. Once you begin to amass material goods, it can be very hard freeing yourself of them. They can begin to trap you and weigh heavily on you. They began to feel like a real burden for me and I started to question their need.

I know of people who have made the decision to just sell everything and go travelling, or to downsize by getting rid of many of their possessions. One friend of mine, upon getting a divorce and moving house, recognised he had so much stuff which he had collected over the years that he had nowhere to put it in his new, smaller house. He made a courageous (and painful) decision to hire a skip and throw out anything that he hadn't used or seen in at least a year. He concluded that if he hadn't touched it in that time, he really didn't need it. He donated some things to charity and sold others, but he most importantly freed himself. Afterwards, he said he felt like a great weight had been lifted off his shoulders, as he no longer had to carry that stuff around with him.

How do you want to be remembered when you finally depart this earth? Do you want to be remembered as someone who had a load of money, a big house, and a posh car? Or do you want people to remember you as someone who was fun to be around and a kind person who loved and cared for others? Now, of course you can have both if you can get that balance right, but don't let materialism become the main focus and reason for what you do in life. When you go to the grave, you ultimately want to go there as someone who was loved by their family and friends. Let's be honest—love is the only thing that really matters.

As humans, our basic desire and need is to be loved and to love someone back. We should want to be measured by the love and joy we brought into this world, not by the collection of wealth and pointless materialistic goods we amassed.

DEFENDING OURSELVES AND THOSE WE LOVE

My mother's life has been filled with a succession of disastrous relationships. In 1981, when I was fourteen, she became involved with a man a few years younger than her who she had met at work. At first he seemed okay, and would take us out for day trips to the seaside. Of course, I now realise this was just him buttering my mum up and portraying himself as a good bloke who liked kids. He had apparently been married before and had left the marriage heavily in debt. After a few months of dating my mum, he finally moved into our home on Doncaster Road in Selby. This was the house that my dad and mum had first bought together when I was four or five years old.

The relationship between me and this man quickly deteriorated. He grew jealous of how close me and my mum were at that time, so he began a campaign of marginalising me and badmouthing me at every opportunity. I would hear him saying uncomplimentary and derogatory things about me to my mum when he didn't think I could hear. He made being in the same room as him so unpleasant and tense that I ended up spending most of my time in my bedroom, listening to my Beatles records, and dreaming of the day I would escape the shit life and the claustrophobic town I lived in. I dreamed of one day becoming a world-famous pop star.

My mum and This Man (I will refer to him only as This Man, as I don't want to mention his name) eventually had two children, both boys—my half-brothers. I am on good terms with the younger of the two, but have no relationship at all with the elder. The same also goes for my mother these days—apart from the odd text message on birthdays and Christmas cards, my mum and I have no real relationship.

In 1984, This Man's job transferred him from Yorkshire, down south to a place called Devizes, in Wiltshire. After a few months of him working down in Devizes, my mum decided to sell the house and move down south as well. I was finally escaping the town of Selby and moving over 200 miles away to a place I had never heard of, into a council flat.

Devizes was like the land that time forgot. For me, it was like moving to another country. I was used to visiting the city of Leeds nearly every weekend to go shopping for clothes and records, or to watch Leeds United. This was during the early 1980s, when the "football-casual" scene exploded across the UK. Young men like myself, who went to watch football, stopped wearing club scarfs and replica shirts and began to wear expensive designer brands of the day, such as Fila, Lacoste, Ralph Lauren, Benetton, Sergio Tacchini, and Pringle, to name but a few. With Leeds only half an hour away from Selby by train, and its abundance of clothes shops selling the latest casual clothing, it was easy for me to immerse myself in the casual scene. When I arrived in Devizes, the casual scene had somehow managed to bypass the town and its neighbouring villages. With my Vinnie Jones haircut and dressed in designer sports brands, I stood out like a sore thumb amongst the locals, and I always seemed to end up in some kind of altercation whenever I went out drinking in the pubs. I did eventually make friends with a few of the locals, and even went out with a few local girls who thought my Yorkshire accent was extremely cool; but I think its fair to say that me and Devizes never really hit it off.

After moving south, I found myself even more isolated. I didn't have my dad or my granny and granddads to escape to for a few hours, away from the awful, tense atmosphere of the flat we were now living in. We did eventually move out of the flat and into a council house in a village called Poulshot, or "Poulshit", as I referred to it. Poulshot was even worse—a village which boasted a pub and a telephone box, and that was it. It was about four miles from Devizes town centre, and had only one bus service into town per day.

The constant snide remarks from This Man continued, and I spent pretty much all of my waking time in my bedroom when he was around. I would hear him and my mum arguing frequently. He behaved like a spoilt child and he had no money sense at all, which led him to get into more debt. The debts from his previous marriage had been wiped clean for him with the money my mum got from the sale of the house. Once we had moved, he again got himself, and, by implication, my mum, in debt. The arguments between them started to get more frequent and he continued to attack me verbally to my mum, thinking I couldn't hear him.

My mother should have protected me from the emotional and psychological abuse I had to endure, but she was weak and she failed. She failed not only to protect me, but also to protect herself. One Sunday morning, everything came to ahead. They were both in their bedroom, arguing again. I had spent years listening to this and was I fed up and emotionally tired of it all. I was tired of listening to my mum screaming and crying and I was sick to the back teeth of hearing his pathetic excuses for his latest fuckup. I was now probably nineteen or twenty years of age by this point, and able to handle myself physically—all the fighting I had been getting up to on a weekend in the town centre and at football had served me well. So on this particular Sunday, I heard the raised voices and my mum getting upset about another "get rich quick" scheme he had bought into that had gone wrong. I heard his pathetic, whining voice spewing out excuses. And I had finally heard enough. I decided that this situation could not carry on; something had to give, or this would just keep happening.

I could hear my mother crying, so I grabbed a sturdy wooden baton I kept in my bedroom for protection, and burst into their bedroom. He was lying on the bed, and I wanted to lay into him there and then.

"Get fucking outside now and I'll kick your fucking head in," I shouted at him. He looked completely shocked. "Come on, outside now, just you and me. Let's fight man to man," I continued.

He declined my offer and I saw genuine fear in his eyes. This Man was a coward of the highest order. For years this bastard had bullied and destroyed not only my mum's confidence but also mine. But I didn't care anymore. I had flipped the switch and now I was going to see this through to its conclusion.

"Get fucking outside now and let's fight," I demanded yet again.

He was frozen to the spot on the bed. The game was up for him and I could see in his eyes that he knew it. He had crossed the line for the last time, and he had crumbled when confronted. I now had the upper hand. He could no longer think he ruled the roost, and with it, me.

My mum was now pleading with me to stop and leave the room, saying she would deal with it.

"He needs to fucking go, Mum. I'm not having him upset you anymore," I told her. She kept pleading for me to leave the room, so I agreed, but I gave him a warning before departing the room. "You upset my mum again, and I will fucking kill ya."

After I left, I returned to my bedroom, shaking not with fear but with anger and adrenaline. I then heard my mum tell him he would have to leave. She had finally found strength to say enough is enough and end the relationship, encouraged through me confronting him.

I had always known that the day would come and we would have an inevitable showdown. I had been very close to confronting him before, but had always pulled myself back at the last second. But this time, I had snapped, the line had been crossed for the last time and it was never going to be crossed again. I had complete confidence in myself and my ability to destroy him physically. He may have been physically taller and much bigger than me, but I knew he was a coward. When confronted, he proved himself as such. Any remaining power he had over my mum disappeared that day.

A few days after the confrontation, he was gone. He packed up and returned to his mother's house in Harrogate, Yorkshire, and I never spoke to him again. For me it was a huge relief. I felt a sense of freedom which I hadn't felt for many years. I was able to walk around the house and not fear bumping into him, I didn't have to listen to the arguing and my mother crying, and I didn't have to hear him verbally attack me to my mum anymore. At last I felt I could breathe, the constant stress of living in such an environment had been lifted. My mum also seemed to be happier, as did my brothers who were still only very young. I helped out with money as best as I could, and neighbours would give my mum lifts into town, as she was now without a car.

Relationships should bring joy and happiness to your life; of course there will be times when it is tough. But if your relationship brings more misery and stress than joy then it is probably time to ask some serious questions and consider getting out.

You can escape. You are allowed to end the relationship. Nobody owns you. You just need to be courageous and strong, and when you say it's over, mean it, and do whatever you need to do to get out and move on. Do not let fear keep you in an unhappy relationship. You deserve to be in a relationship where you are valued, loved, and treated with respect. And ultimately you deserve happiness.

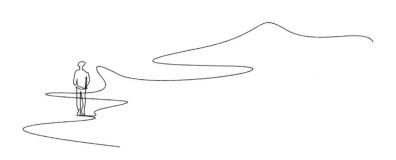

TRUE HEROES

The past few years, with the COVID-19 pandemic spreading across the world and effectively closing it down, normal life as we know it has been put on hold. For me personally, this meant I was unable to go to Australia to watch the England cricket team in the T20 World Cup. This was a trip I had planned a year in advance and for which I had paid my deposit and booked out the time in my diary. I was also unable to make my usual Christmas trip to Lanzarote for a spot of winter sunshine. But apart from these issues, I am fortunate that the lockdowns have affected me very little.

For many, not being able to go out and mix in large groups, visit family and friends, and attend concerts and sporting events has been difficult. Had COVID happened when I was in my twenties, then my thoughts on the pandemic may have been somewhat different, due to the effects it would have had on my social life. I do sympathise with young people, and I've seen it affect both my daughters in that respect. My youngest daughter was not able to celebrate her twenty-first birthday as she would have wanted to do with her friends—in a club dancing the night away.

COVID has certainly helped us more easily identify the selfish people within our society—those who feel entitled and that the rules do not apply to them. Since I began writing this in 2020, we now know the UK's very own Prime Minister Boris Johnson believed himself to be above the law, and was partying in Downing Street with his colleagues. The man and his government who wrote the laws broke them continuously. There has also been an emergence of conspiracy theorists, "anti-maskers" and "anti-vaxxers", as they have become known, who despite having no relevant qualifications, suddenly believe they are experts in all things medical and scientific, and are all too eager to let their non-expert, non-credibly researched views be known across social media.

One of the most sickening things for me during the crisis has been watching President of the United States Donald Trump encourage these conspiracy theorists by downplaying the threat of COVID and publicly berating those who wear face masks. He even attacked the world-renowned immunologist and Chief Medical Advisor to the President, Dr Anthony Fauci, for reporting facts and advising the public of the very real dangers of the pandemic.

Apart from highlighting those who are selfish and uncaring, COVID has also shown us the good in society. For me, those National Health Service staff who put themselves on the front line and in danger's way to look after those who succumbed to the virus represent the very best of humanity. In fact, all the "key workers", those who kept the essential services running, deserve our thanks. COVID has shown us who the true heroes in our society are, and it has highlighted just how vital those workers are who are usually given little thought. Without these people, society would quite literally fall apart.

It isn't the self-obsessed famous-for-nothing YouTubers and reality TV stars we should be admiring, but the refuse workers, lorry drivers, shop workers, fruit and vegetable pickers, delivery drivers, postmen and women, healthcare workers, care-home staff, bakers, food-production workers, police, firefighters, ambulance drivers, pharmacists, and all public-service workers. These are the real heroes, the people who society normally undervalues; they keep society going. Without them, we'd grind to a halt and crumble into chaos and anarchy. Yet, it seems to me that we pay those who contribute most to society the least, and those who contribute least to society the most.

Imagine for one moment a society without the refuse worker, or the "bin men", as they are more commonly known. For years, these great public servants have been the butt of jokes, looked down on, mocked, and ridiculed by those who believe they are superior to someone who empties bins for a living. They assume they must be stupid. All of this is patently untrue. Imagine just how awful life would be without these people—they are absolutely crucial to society and yet we barely notice them or give them a thought. We just take them for granted, putting our full bins out in the morning and returning from work to empty ones, without ever stopping to be grateful. I have read reports from refuse collectors about the abuse from drivers they get when the collection vehicles block the streets as they go about their vital role. Some impatient arseholes have even assaulted refuse collectors for merely doing their job.

As we move into a post-COVID world, let's hear it for the bin men and women of our nation, and all those other undervalued, poorly paid and largely forgotten working-class heroes. Let's not forget just how crucial these people are to our everyday lives, and show them gratitude when you get the opportunity. A simple but genuine "Thank you" to the person delivering your next parcel, or just asking the till person how their day is going and showing an interest in them on a human level, can make such a difference to that individual's day. These little acts of kindness and appreciation shown to others really matter and do make a difference. Whenever I am the recipient of such an act of appreciation, it restores my faith in humanity.

And please, while I am at it, can I ask that we stop the ridiculous worship of social media "influencers" and reality TV stars? Please understand that what they portray to you is only a fantasy designed to get likes and views, which in turn earns them money. There is nothing real about reality TV stars; it is all heavily choreographed and edited.

I also want you to understand that what people post on social media is only the bits of their life which they want to show you, usually the bits where they are pretending to have a great time. You will be familiar with the quote that usually goes alongside some picture of them on the beach, or at a concert—*Living my best life.* What they rarely show you, if ever, are the really crap times they have. I personally love the quote, *May your life be as truly awesome as you pretend it is on social media.*

Be you, don't try to be anyone else, you are beautiful as you are, you don't need the latest designer bag, made from the skin of some murdered rare exotic animal, to be important. You already are important to lots of people, people who really matter, not people on social media.

ENJOY THE RIDE

From a young age, I always knew that the mundane life of a normal nine-to-five job was not for me. I always dreamed of more, and I knew that life didn't have to be what school tried to condition and brainwash me into accepting.

My peers told me if I got a good factory job, played my cards right, and kissed the right arses, I could become a foreman. That was the extent of the ambition that many of those I grew up around had. But I instinctively realised that I didn't have to accept a life spent on a factory floor. I didn't want to spend decades slogging my guts out for a pittance of pay, and for a company that really didn't give a flying fuck if I lived or died. Let's face it, we are all replaceable to those in power. There are always plenty more wretches like me being churned out by the comprehensive school system from which I came. The ruling classes have always seen the working class as mere cannon fodder. One only has to read the history of the coal mines and the First World War to see this played out.

No, thank you, that life wasn't for me.

Even so, I was surrounded by people whose lives seemed to be going nowhere fast, if anywhere at all; they lived lives of just...

existing. The rat race had them truly ensnared. They had bought fully into the dream of consumerism and acceptance of a system that made them slaves for the rest of their lives.

Be grateful; don't get above your station.

Buy a new colour TV, bigger than the last one.

Buy a faster car.

Go on holiday once a year.

If you were really lucky, a holiday would be to somewhere like Torremolinos, after which you would return home with tales of Spanish waiters, sunburn, topless sunbathers, food poisoning, cheap beer, tacky gifts, and maybe a sexual disease. This seemed to be the dream fed to my generation of snotty-nosed, working-class kids. My response: Fuck that!

I decided my life was going to be full of interesting people, the arts, writing, singing, politics, and all the things that "my type" of people didn't get involved in.

I was often told, "That stuff is not for the likes of us."

Luckily, my dad was different. He was a bit of an outsider; he was an artist and I must say a bloody good one as well, even if I am biased. He had gone to York College of Art as a mature student in his mid-twenties, and he was also extremely politically minded. As a young man, he had been one of the original Ban the Bomb marchers of the early 1960s, taking part in the London to Aldermaston CND marches. (Aldermaston, at that time, was where the UK's atomic weapons research centre was.) Listening to my dad talk politics had a massive influence on my life. His own irreverence towards those in power made me realise that I didn't have to blindly accept; I could question, and I didn't have to be like everyone else. I could look beyond the factory floor, and I could have my own opinions and express them.

He taught me that I didn't have to just accept what was

supposedly mapped out for me. I could be brave.

It is fair to say that my dad was a bit of a childhood hero to me. Although he left home when I was eight years old, I still saw him every weekend, and as a youngster I idolised him. I even forgave his appalling behaviour when he was drunk, excusing it as "just the way artistic people are," and seeing it as part of his "tortured genius". As I matured, I began to realise my dad was like any other person when drunk—an arsehole; no excuses. He was just like the many other arseholes in this world who can't handle their drink. They become pains in the arse, and bores.

Despite my high hopes, there wasn't much for me straight out of school. I was living in the small Yorkshire town of Selby. Selby was at the heart of the new Yorkshire coalfields, with a number of super-pits located around the area. Soon after leaving school, the miners went on strike, so there was even less work to be found there. I signed on the dole and became just another one of "Maggie's millions" as the unemployed had become known.

I briefly ended up on a Youth Training Scheme (YTS) which was, in reality, a bit of cheap labour for many firms. The government would pay the YTS employee £25 a week for a year whilst they worked full-time for a local firm. Then, at the end of the year, many would find that there was no full-time job available and be back on the dole. Meanwhile, the company would then employ another YTS skivvy to replace them. I only lasted a few weeks on the YTS scheme before getting kicked off for constantly messing about. At one point I thought it would be fun to lock another YTS worker in a cupboard, and despite his desperate pleas I didn't let him out. Me and my fellow YTS employees all thought it was hilarious. It was only after much shouting for help that one of the charge-hands heard him and opened the door. I couldn't take the thing seriously, and I wasn't prepared to be used and taken advantage of, so it was back on the dole.

Thatcher's Britain was in full swing; the booming London yuppie set filled the wine bars of the city, drove their Porsches, and bought their luxury dockland apartments. This was a million miles from the life of myself and my mates in 1980s Britain. For us, and many like us, our realities were football, drinking, girls, and fighting.

As previously mentioned I had just turned seventeen when my mum and her new partner moved us all south to Devizes. I stuck out like a sore thumb in the sleepy rural town.

I didn't know anyone, but I had a Lambretta scooter and was into the mod scene, so this eventually helped me make friends with a few similar people. I began to regularly visit Swindon which was the nearest big town, just over twenty miles away. Swindon seemed to be the only place nearby that had any kind of life and semblance of style. Devizes didn't even have a train station, and the bus service was poor, to say the least. If you didn't have your own transport, then you were pretty much stuck in the one-horse, dead-end, backward town. (Sorry if this upsets anyone from Devizes, but this was the early 80s and it was a very inward-looking place back then. Outsiders like me were viewed with suspicion.)

It was while living in Devizes that I was introduced to what passed as excitement for some of the local lads: a good end to a weekend night out was to go "squaddie bashing", as they referred to it.

Devizes was surrounded by army camps, with Salisbury Plain's military training ranges just up the road. Friday and Saturday nights would see groups of young squaddies come into town—fuck knows why, because there really was nothing there—there were no clubs and everything closed at 11p.m. This invasion of outsiders chatting up the local girls and drinking in "their pubs" would upset some of the local six-fingered monsters who, after downing as much Wadsworth's beer as they possibly could before closing time, would vow to defend the local female population from the attention of the young army lads. After kicking-out time, the locals would pick fights with the young squaddies. I witnessed countless drunken fights by the large fountain in the centre of town, and ended up in a fair few myself.

I was also the target of numerous locals because of my thick Yorkshire accent, fashionable clothes, and the fact I only had the usual five digits on each hand. (I am merely jesting about the number of fingers the locals had, of course.) With all this being classed as a "good night out" in Devizes, I took myself to Swindon most weekends, which was positively cosmopolitan in comparison. The locals were accepting of people from other areas of the UK who didn't happen to speak like country bumpkins. Swindon at the time was a booming town, with many national and international companies moving their offices there due to its great access to London and Bristol.

While living in Devizes, I did get my first ever proper job, working in a local jam factory. This job gave me my first taste of having my own money, and I did meet some really nice people there. The job itself was depressing, and it gave me my first glimpse of a world that I desperately wanted to avoid. I met people who were married with kids and who were slaves to the wage. People whose whole lives revolved around their job. It defined who they were, and most hated it, but they were trapped—or at least they believed they were trapped. They were too afraid to leave the security it offered no matter how much they detested the bosses and the work. During the lunch breaks, these workers would often tell me of their dreams, of winning the football pools and escaping the factory floor. They fantasised about one day doing a job they enjoyed which allowed them to use the true talents they possessed.

I would sit there, listening to their dreams, and even back then at the age of seventeen I thought, "Why not just leave this place?" It made me feel sad to listen to them, and I vowed that this was never going to be my story.

What kept those workers in that job, instead of pursuing their dreams, was FEAR.

It is probably a good time again to repeat the quote from American psychologist Abraham Maslow who said the following:

"We fear our highest possibilities. We are generally afraid to become that which we can glimpse in our most perfect moments, under conditions of great courage. We enjoy and even thrill to godlike possibilities we see in ourselves in such peak moments. And yet we simultaneously shiver with weakness, awe, and fear before these very same possibilities."

Nothing changes until you change. Only when you change what you are doing and thinking will things start to fall into place. Think about it—it's so obvious, isn't it? How can you expect anything to change if you don't change? It's like setting the cruise control on your car to 60mph, then expecting your car to suddenly travel at 70mph without changing anything. It's never going to happen. You have to reset and change your own settings in life.

• • •

There I was, living in Devizes and hating it. I lived for a short time in Swindon, and I also briefly moved back up to Selby, but things hadn't worked out, and I found myself back at my mum's in Devizes, going nowhere fast, feeling lost. I was becoming more and more depressed and desperately looking for a way out. It was early 1989, and I knew I was ready to make a serious change in my life.

I didn't have the financial clout to rent my own place, as I had no full time job at the time. The beautiful city of Bath was about twenty miles up the road from Devizes and it seemed appealing. I knew it was a tourist city, but I didn't know much else about it. When I had visited Bath I felt it had a nice feel and vibe, so I decided I would try to move there and get a job. As it turned out, although I didn't realise it at the time, this one decision would change my entire life. It never ceases to amaze me how seemingly insignificant decisions can end up completely rewriting the course of your whole life. For me that is an exciting concept. No matter where you are in life right now, you have the power to change direction.

I decided to try for a job in a hotel, since I had heard that hotels often gave staff live-in accommodation. I got out the Yellow Pages (no internet in those days), and began looking up hotels in Bath and ringing round a few. Eventually, I rang a three-star hotel called The Lansdown Grove Hotel, and after speaking with the manager, I managed to get an interview for a porter's job.

When I turned up for the interview, I was taken aback by the hotel. It was like nothing I had seen before. It seemed huge and extremely posh. I met with the manager, Mr. Thomas, who explained to me what the job entailed, the weekly wage (after deductions for food), and most importantly for me, the live-in accommodation. I must have said the right things and given him the right impression, because I was offered the job and I happily accepted.

This one action, as I have already stated, changed my whole life, and I do not say that lightly. I can look back now, some thirty years on, and see how moving to Bath brought me to where I am today. It got me out of my depressing existence in Devizes and allowed me to earn some money. But more importantly, I was suddenly thrust into an environment where a lot of the people working in the hotel were just like me—trying to find their way in life.

The hotel industry seemed to attract a lot of lost people. Young people like me, searching for escape and freedom, and older men in particular who had broken marriages and relationships, and were looking for a new start, just like me. The hotel offered accommodation, food, and wages. There was also a massive drinking culture within the industry, along with a lot of casual sex amongst staff, which, being a young man in my early twenties, I embraced fully.

I was twenty-one when I first walked through the doors of The Lansdown Grove Hotel. The staff team was made up of people from all over the world, and the hotel guests came from many different countries to visit the heritage city of Bath. Working in this multicultural environment opened up my eyes completely. If people could travel to Bath from other countries, not knowing anyone, and start to build a life for themselves, then I could also do anything I wanted to do. They showed me that anything was possible. I learned that, yes, they did have fears about travelling, but they didn't let fear win, they did it anyway.

I fell in love with the city of Bath and the nightlife, the people, the architecture—everything about it still holds a very special place in my heart to this day.

It was whilst working at the hotel that I met an Australian girl who had started working there shortly after me, and with whom I fell madly in love. For me, this would be the first time I had truly fallen for anyone. I thought I had been in love at least once before, but I soon realised that what I thought had been love really wasn't. I was completely head-over-heels in love with this girl, though I initially tried to deny it. Eventually, I could deny it no longer and I had to throw caution to the wind. I was prepared to accept whatever my fate was to be in the hands of love.

She moved into the flat which the hotel provided for me, and we had a beautiful year together. During this time, I experienced the most intense feelings I had ever known up to that point in my life, and it scared the shit out of me, as well as making me start to re-evaluate a lot of the assumptions I had about many things, from religion to morals.

I also met an American guy called Mark, who was also working as a porter, and we became good friends. It is fair to say before I met Mark, my opinion of Americans generally was pretty low. I had thought of them as brash and loud, money-obsessed and vulgar (think of the episode of the British comedy *Fawlty Towers*, where the American tourist visits the hotel and complains about the roads being too small, the British weather, and the Mickey Mouse money). Mark was none of those things, and we became such good friends that after he returned to Los Angeles, I went out there to visit him for a number of weeks. I also made friends with his brother, Ted, who remains a good friend of mine to this day and who I still meet up with whenever he visits Bath.

I eventually left my job in the hotel in September of 1989, after returning from my extended stay in the USA, where as well as getting drunk pretty much every night, I did some promoting of my second record, a four-track EP called *North in the South*, I even shot a promotional video for one of the songs whilst in LA (but that's another story).

I remained in Bath, finding another hotel job which, although it did not offer me live-in accommodation, paid part of the rent for a room in a shared house. My landlady, Pat, was like a second mum to me. When I lost my second hotel job, she didn't charge me rent for a few weeks and helped me get a new job as a social worker. This led me to meet my wife, who was also a social worker, and the rest, as they say, is history.

What started as a thought and an acknowledgment that things needed to change for me, led to that one decision to move to Bath in 1989, which changed everything. Had I remained in Devizes, I dread to think how my life may have turned out. I wouldn't have met my wife (one of my luckiest breaks), which means I wouldn't have had my beautiful daughters, and gone on to experience all the wonderful things I have from being a father. Just recounting this very brief history amazes me as I begin to join the dots of how I got to where I am today.

One seemingly small decision can change your present reality, and with it, the whole course of your life. You just need the courage to take those first steps and move into the frequency of that which you desire.

So what are you waiting for? Be brave, put on your big boy/girl pants, and take up the challenge to change if you feel like your life is going nowhere fast.

What have you got to lose? You can either stay where you are, unfulfilled, empty, and miserable, or you can take that leap of faith, strap in, and enjoy the ride.

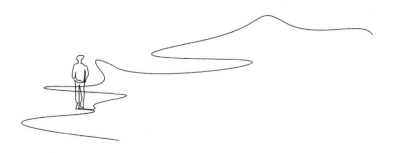

TRUE FRIENDS

The things I once found entertaining or of importance in my life have changed over time. Some might call this an "enlightenment", which sounds very New Age, but it is true. Enlightenment for me started by shining a light on all aspects of my life, this involved scrutinizing, questioning and really examining everything I believed. As I did this it became very clear that I was no longer the person I was still acting out as. I was playing the part that people expected of me, the part I had been playing for years. Shining light and examining everything, enabled me to expose what was false within me, and so began the internal clear out. I knew I needed to change, to turn the page and start to be the person I was now.

I could see the futility of violence and the pettiness and ridiculousness of so many of the things which used to anger and upset me.

The moment I turned the page, I began to see new worlds and possibilities, while my old friends and acquaintances remained stuck on the previous page. They were still talking about the same things, working the same jobs, in the same relationships, angry at the world, and continuing to blame others for whatever shit they were experiencing. Ultimately, they were still taking no responsibility for their own lives. They couldn't see that they are responsible for everything good and bad that happens to them.

When you make the decision to make changes to your life, you will undoubtedly be faced with friends, acquaintances, and maybe even family members trying to dissuade you from doing so. They will appear to be concerned that you are about to make a huge mistake, and will be only too happy to reel off a million and one reasons why you shouldn't be embarking on a journey of change. They will encourage you to remain as you are, even if it is miserable, unhappy, and unfulfilled, because at least it is safe. What they will fail to see or recognise is the huge potential and positives which are possible from change.

The truth is, they are fearful; not necessarily for you, but for themselves. They have lied to themselves for so many years and convinced themselves that change isn't possible. They have countless well rehearsed excuses and reasons why this is the case. Yet here you are, enlightened and excited at the potential that awaits you as you take that first step outside of the familiar.

You are willing to take that leap of faith, knowing that there is another world, another life outside of the narrow confines that you presently find yourself trapped in.

It is this potential that poses a threat to many of those around you. If you go on your journey and succeed, it will shine a light on their reality and expose the lies they have told themselves about change not being possible. You will suddenly become living proof that a different world and life is possible, and they can no longer claim that life is shit and you can't change it, because as we know, you can.

During your process of change, old friends and acquaintances will begin to drop you like hot coals. You will also find that you begin removing yourself from some people because your relationship with them no longer serves you. In my case, it wasn't because I disliked these people, but because I was no longer on the same frequency as them. By turning the page to a new chapter in your life, you expose a new reality—which has always existed, waiting for you to discover it, but only now because you have gone in search of that new reality can it come to light.

Once I started my journey, I found that whenever I met up with old friends and acquaintances, I entered briefly back into what was once my world, and elements of this world sickened me. I could no longer accept the heavy drinking and the talk of violence and hatred. Seeing and hearing the people who I had spent years in the company of, was like seeing my old self reflected back at me. It was no longer what I wanted to identify with, and my old ways made me feel ashamed. Boastful talk of drinking to excess, random acts of violence, racism, and misogyny was no longer what I wanted to be around—and in truth, it never really was.

When I declined to join in on the drinks rounds and explained that I didn't wish to drink to excess, they looked at me as if I had grown two heads. I was mocked and ridiculed because, in their world, to be a true man meant you had to drink to excess. If you didn't drink yourself into a bumbling, shit-talking moron, then you must have become some kind of "raging homosexual". (I use this example merely to point out the macho bullshit of the world I once inhabited. I personally have nothing against the gay community at all. Love is love.) This was a reminder of what I formerly surrounded myself with; a shallow world of emptiness, devoid of any true meaning, where the only deep conversation is of next week's football trip and pub visits.

Expect to lose people along the way. Some will just naturally fall away and out of your life. At the same time, you will also find new friends and acquaintances who truly support you, and who will continue to be there encouraging you as you climb to new heights. Life is a journey where you are continually moving and learning. As such, you are presented with a constantly changing landscape.

Your true friends will remain loyal and support you. True friends will never try to discourage you from what you are setting out to do—unless it is incredibly blatant and obviously detrimental to you, and in that case, any discouragement will only be through genuine concern and love for you.

When I decided that being involved in the football hooligan scene was no longer for me, I received a fair bit of abuse, dressed up as banter. I would still go to games, but I would not get involved in the heavy drinking, the provoking of arguments and fights, and abusive chanting. For me, enough was enough. There were people who took offence at my unwillingness to be involved in the behaviour they were still partaking in. Some just couldn't handle the fact I wasn't acting an arsehole or drinking myself into a slurring mess and looking for trouble.

On one occasion, I was drinking in a pub pre-game with the usual crowd. The pub was getting more crowded, to the point where you couldn't hold a conversation due to the noise and you had to wait an age to get a drink. In days gone by, I would have tolerated and even enjoyed the fact the pub was so full, and I would definitely have been right at the forefront of any chanting. But this heaving, sweating, beer-swilling mass of humanity was just not fun anymore for me, so I told one of the lads I was going to find a quieter pub. Half an hour later, after finding a much quieter spot, I received an aggressive text from one particular lad in our group asking where I was and telling me he was pissed off because I had come out with them and had now gone.

I asked him why this had upset him. Wasn't he able to survive without me being in the pub with him? There were plenty of others from our group in the pub with him, so what was his problem? After a few more angry texts from him, I decided to hit the issue on the head and tell him straight.

I texted him back, telling him I didn't want to fall out with him, but if he carried on sending such texts we *would* be falling out, and this would be of his own making. I told him to stop worrying about me and enjoy his drinking with everyone else. This did the trick; he knew that my text was alluding to the fact that the situation could end up getting physical if he continued to push me. He also knew that, despite all of the drunken courage he presently displayed, he really didn't want to be getting into a fight with me.

It's fair to say I lost a lot of my old football mates once I decided to take myself away from the madness. Some people just can't handle seeing you change. But you shouldn't shed any tears over losing those people. It is nothing personal; they just no longer add any value to your life. While they remain stuck in their limited world, you are expanding yours. True friends will grow along with you and support your journey.

RAISING A FAMILY AND
DREAMS ON PAUSE

For the last twenty-five years, during which I have focused on how to best provide for my family, my life in some areas has felt like it is on pause. My time has been spent concentrating on earning a living, often working in jobs that bored me senseless and made me feel worthless, wasted, unmotivated, depressed, and resentful. (Yep, it's fair to say I hated most of my jobs.)

I was only suffering through these jobs because they paid a wage and I needed to provide for my children. I had brought them into this world, and it was my job to ensure they felt loved, clothed, and had a roof over their heads and food in their bellies.

I wanted them to have all the things I never had growing up. Stability, holidays, fun, and, above all, I wanted them to feel secure and protected. Security was something that I never felt after the age of eight, when my father left the family home. Giving my daughters a feeling of security was of such huge importance to me, I was willing to put on pause any ambitions of my own.

You often hear parents say they want to give their kids everything they never had. When people talk about this, they are quite often referring to material things. For me, I always meant all-embracing love and security. Providing that security meant providing a home, which meant paying a mortgage and bills, which meant I had to work jobs I hated and, as already stated, put my own personal desires on the back burner.

Life, just like a book, has chapters. The length of each chapter is determined by what you are doing, and within each chapter there are smaller sub-chapters. Within the all-encompassing story of your life, there are lots of other smaller stories going on at the same time.

Let me explain what I mean by this. So, the big, all-encompassing story at this time of your life may be bringing up a family; within that will be the story of your marriage. At the same time as those stories are going on, there will be the story of your work, which involves relationships with colleagues or customers etc. So lots of little stories are being played out all at the same time within the big story.

Looking at the last twenty-five years of my life as a chapter, I have been on a huge learning curve. The lessons have been many, and I'm still learning them. One lesson learned is that materialism and possessions do not make you happy; they are not the path to true happiness, and they actually weigh you down and can keep you anchored to the spot. Another lesson I have learned is one about love and service, putting others' needs before my own. I have very often served my children and my wife's needs before my own. I do not regret doing so one bit, as this is what was needed of me at the time. And I am sure if you asked my wife, she would also say she has put mine and our girls' needs before her own.

I played the cards I was dealt at the time in the best way I could. Maybe in hindsight, I would have played some cards differently, but we all know we cannot change the past. I played the hands I was dealt, with no guidance whatsoever; in effect, making it up as I went along. I had no self-help books to reference, no YouTube videos or websites to turn to when I was struggling. Admittedly, these resources can never give you the ultimate answer to anything, but they can give you food for thought and help you to see things from a different perspective. They can offer support and reassurance that you are not alone in thinking and feeling the way you do. I had none of that, and I felt completely alone much of the time. I felt that I couldn't go to my friends and admit any weakness, for fear I would be laughed at and ridiculed.

Things are (thankfully) very different today. My past experiences of feeling alone and of being totally out of my depth inspired me to write this book.

If you are also going through the process of bringing up a family, I would like to remind you that you are important as well. Don't lose who you are in what can seem like the chaos and constant dramas of family life. You can still find time for you and the things you desire, and you can still pursue your personal goals without having to feel guilty. Remember that you matter, and that being unhappy and miserable does not serve your family in the long run, as it will affect everyone else. Never lose sight of who you are.

There are more chapters to come in the book of your life, and it is up to you to write them as best as you can.

As I sit here writing these lines, analysing the past, I realise that I may have put my life and my dreams on pause, but my desires have always remained within me. I just buried them deep inside, keeping them under wraps, ready to be unpacked another day, in another chapter.

Author Anaïs Nin wrote the following words, which I feel encapsulate that feeling perfectly: "And the day came when the risk to remain tight in a bud was more painful than the risk it took to blossom."

Much like this, the day came for me when the desire and calling within me became so overwhelming that I found myself on the precipice, desperately wanting to leap off the edge and leave my fate to the Universe. I concluded that I had two options: be brave and jump, or stay where I was and slowly wither and die. I decided to be brave and trust in the Universe. I leapt.

I leapt with all my fucking might and I closed my eyes and I prayed and I handed my fate over to God/the Universe/the Source Energy/whatever you wish to call it. I just trusted that a power far bigger than me would catch me and take me to exactly where I needed to be.

I showed by jumping that I was ready for change and that I was serious in wanting it. The Universe caught me, took me under its wing, and delivered me safely to my next chapter.

Until I had my own children, I never knew it was possible to feel such a deep love for anyone. I realised very quickly that every decision I made no longer only affected me, but it also affected the three other people in my family. I learned not to be self-obsessed. As someone who naturally likes his own company, I learned how to live within a family, make joint decisions, compromise, and budget. I learned so many lessons which were truly beautiful. But, as wonderful as all this was, I also realise now that I lost sight of who I was as I focused on the task of providing for my family and being the best dad I could be, which is an admirable thing. But I ended up burying my true calling to write, whether that be songs or scripts, plays or books.

Before the pause which saw me solely focused on providing for my family, I was in the music business trying to make a name for myself. This was the late 1980s, and during this time, amongst many other things going on in my life, I released two records.

(Those of a certain age reading this will know what I mean when I say "records". I'm talking about the round, black, vinyl variety, which were played on a record player using a needle and would often jump around and played with a crackle and hiss before the actual music began.)

Writing songs was something I felt drawn to and compelled to do for over twenty years, and even now, I will every so often get a tune and a few lines of lyrics in my head which are too good for me to ignore. I record them onto my phone, telling myself one day I will go back into the recording studio and record them properly. My days of becoming a pop star are probably over, but that doesn't mean someone younger who still has the looks and the energy can't record my songs and potentially have a hit. Even so, my writing focus these days has changed from writing songs to writing scripts and books.

Now, as my beautiful children are older and have gone out into the big wide world themselves, I realise a new and exciting chapter (predominately about me) is about to be written. When we come to these moments in our life, we need to remember that how we fill the pages within this new chapter is in our own hands. The story we write will be largely determined by how brave we are in taking those leaps of faith required and not letting fear dictate. We need to be the ruling force that writes the chapter of our dreams.

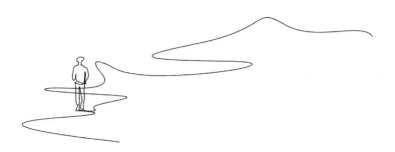

THE PAST IS NEVER FAR BEHIND

When I was seventeen, I embarked on a life of crime. Okay, I exaggerate. But I did embark on a mad few weeks of crime which (embarrassingly) saw me break into my old school, a factory, and a wood yard. I was unemployed at the time; it was the early 80s, and I had just left school and joined the ranks of Maggie's Millions—as the jobless were then known.

In the small, northern industrial town where I grew up, jobs were as rare as hen's teeth. As a seventeen-year-old with no previous work experience, my chances of employment were slim, to say the least. I was a mod back then and had a Vespa scooter, which I needed money to be able to run. That's where the idea to break into my old school came from.

Me and my mate (also a mod with a scooter to run) decided it would be a good idea to break into our old school and pinch the petty cash. Being the complete criminal novices we were, we broke a large window to gain access to the deputy head's office. Once the window was broken, we entered the office and went through the desk drawers. Our hopes of coming across lots of money was short-lived. In total, our booty amounted to a few measly pounds—less than ten pounds each when divided between the two of us. Hardly the riches we had dreamed of.

The morning after the school break-in, I heard the news that my partner in crime had been arrested and was now being questioned by police. It turned out he had been spotted near the school by someone who knew him, and they had reported him to the police after hearing about the break-in. Within hours of his arrest, the police were also at my door arresting me.

I was put in handcuffs, led out of the front door, and placed in the waiting police car—all in full view of the neighbours. Oh, the shame of it all.

I had never been arrested before, and other than the odd bit of shoplifting from Boots and Woolworths as a child, I had never knowingly committed a crime before either. It turns out my mate, once arrested and questioned, had sung like a canary. He had given my name as his partner in crime, as well as a detailed account of all our crimes, which totalled three.

Once at the police station, I was photographed, fingerprinted, and thrown in a cell for a few hours before being taken out for questioning. I was then subjected to the classic good cop/bad cop routine.

"It's best to get it all off your chest, son. Tell us everything, then you can make a clean start. You're not really a criminal," Good Cop told me.

Then Bad Cop chimed in with, "I don't believe this is the first time you've committed burglaries. We know you've done other stuff and we are gonna charge you with that as well. So make it easier on yourself and tell us now what other stuff you've done."

"I haven't done anything else," I protested.

"Listen, it's no good lying. We have people who can identify you just by a shoe print, so if you confess to the other stuff now, we will just have them taken into consideration," Bad Cop replied.

Bad Cop then began to read out a long list of unsolved burglaries which I genuinely had nothing to do with, but which he wanted me to admit to so he could clear up his unsolved crimes list.

"But I haven't done them," I insisted again. "All I have done are the ones you already know about."

I was then thrown back in the cells for a few more hours before being charged with the break-ins I had committed and released on bail. The worst was yet to come; being arrested and locked up in a cell was nothing in comparison to having to go home and face the shame of what I had done.

My dad had been told about my arrest, as had my granddad and grandma. I felt more ashamed for the fact I had disappointed my granddad and grandma than anything else, as they were good, honest, working-class people. No one in our family had done anything like this before, to my knowledge.

It was a few weeks after my arrest that me, my mum, her boyfriend, and my two very young brothers all moved south to the town of Devizes in Wiltshire. A few months after moving, I had to return to Selby to appear in court. After pleading guilty, I was given a fine and a warning from the magistrate that next time I would be sent to a young offenders' institute. The relief I felt that I didn't go to prison was immense, and I travelled back by train to Devizes in a joyous mood, a free man with his life still before him.

These crimes were all committed nearly forty years ago, have long since become spent, and were committed as a seventeen-year-old juvenile, but to this day they occasionally come back to haunt me. The most recent instance was when I applied for a tourist visa to Australia, where the application process clearly asks you to declare any crime you have been convicted of, even if they are spent convictions.

To me, those past mistakes are a source of major embarrassment and shame. But the seventeen-year-old version of me is not who I am now, and it seems unfair that I should still be having to explain and declare something I did some forty years ago as a kid. Even so, this is my karma returning, and we all must atone for our crimes.

For the record, I was eventually granted my tourist visa for Australia.

STRESS

I have never been one for small talk, although I can do it, if I really must. I struggle with the whole inane falseness of "polite conversation" with some people, and having to fake interest in whatever is being talked about. In truth, I really couldn't give a fuck what little Johnny has been up to recently, and I'm really not interested in listening to the latest holiday adventures or the saga of a new loft conversion and problems with the builders. I find the whole thing incredibly boring and at times hugely stressful. However, I sometimes wish I could find small talk easier, and feel relaxed when in unfamiliar company.

When I met my wife I was thrust into the whole family gathering routine. It was expected that I would go to family Sunday lunches at her parents' house and attend family get-to-gethers, which seemed to be a regular occurrence. The lead-up to such occasions would see me stressed out, and filled with fear at the prospect of having to make small talk with people I didn't really know or seem to have much in common with.

Another Christmas arrived, and I found myself at yet another family gathering with my wife's family. I took my place around the table surrounded by family, and because small talk is something

I find incredibly difficult, sitting there at the table I felt like the proverbial spare prick at a wedding. I doubted they had much interest in my life and what I was doing, so why pretend? After the family gathering was over, I decided that was it for me; I was no longer going to put myself through the stress, anxiety, and complete agony of another Christmas gathering. It wasn't like they would miss me if I didn't turn up I thought.

I imagined they would probably be thinking, "Thank fuck we don't have to put up with him this year." Despite the inevitable and understandable backlash from my wife, I found the courage to say "no", and never attended another Christmas gathering.

I did feel guilty the first few years, as my wife would come up with numerous excuses why I wasn't able to attend. After several years of non attendance, they just accepted that I wouldn't be there. I would be half heartedly asked every year, and I would decline the invitation, which would then incur the wrath of my wife for not supporting her at family events. This was completely understandable, and I did feel incredible guilt about it. All she wanted was her husband to support her, to be there like all the other partners.

I wished, in many ways, I could have been able to sit in a room and engage in the trivial small talk. But that just isn't me, and this whole book is about being authentic and true to yourself. It is about finding who you truly are, as painful as that may be at times.

You are an adult in charge of everything you do and think. As an adult, you are allowed to say "no" to things you do not want to do and which will cause you stress. It took me many years to realise this. My inner child still felt that I wasn't in charge of me and my life, and that I did not have the right to say no.

As you begin to take charge and make your own decisions, you must expect and prepare for the inevitable backlash from those who you are saying no to. Your decisions will not always be popular, and they may not wish to try and understand. But this is your life, and you have the right to make the choices and decisions which you feel serve you best. Do not be bullied into doing something you do not want to do.

I talk a lot in this book about pushing boundaries and challenging yourself; and it is good to get out of your comfort zone and feel the discomfort of growth. But the kind of toxic stress and anxiety I am talking about here causes illness. Severe stress and anxiety are proven to weaken the body's immune system, making you susceptible to ill health. When you are suffering from severe stress, all the toxicity it produces goes coursing through your body and, if it is not released, it ends up settling and causing physical damage and illness. This stress is what I define as "corrosive stress", which is why I say again, you must make decisions which are in your best interest. You and your health matter.

One of the most stressful events in my life was the breakup of my marriage, and the separation. I was leaving a relationship which I had been in for over thirty years. The marriage had become stale, it wasn't exciting anymore for either of us, but it was safe, and it was what we both knew. But I was bored. I was fed up of watching my life pass me by, year after year, and nothing changing. I would secretly hope I could find the courage to be truthful and tell my wife I wanted to leave, but I was a coward and let fear rule me. I had huge dreams of what I would and could be doing with my life if I left. Yet I stayed, remaining unhappy and bored. I was also extremely angry and fearful as I watched the years and my life slipping away during those last few years of being together.

The ridiculousness of the whole situation kept slapping me in the face. Here I was, a man who would happily fight anyone in the boxing ring. I was a self-defence instructor, supposedly tough, yet too afraid to talk honestly with my wife about how I felt because I knew it would be an uncomfortable conversation with difficult repercussions. Although I felt like I wanted out of the relationship, a part of me was extremely scared of breaking the ties and being on my own again. Even though I felt suffocated and increasingly resentful about the whole situation, I let my fear of the unknown keep me from leaving. In my mind I wrongly blamed my wife for my predicament when, in reality, it was of my own making. My choices had got me to where I was, and it was my inability to be honest that kept me there. As my daughters got older, the excuse of my girls still being young and at home was no longer a valid reason to stay in a relationship where I felt unhappy and unfulfilled.

As time went by, my unhappiness grew. We did very little together as a couple; my wife did her thing and I would do mine, and the stress of the whole situation just grew. I would bottle it up inside me until I could release it by weight training in my gym, or through hitting the punch bag or sparring. I could literally feel the stress building inside me, making me sick. Something had to give, which it inevitably did when we both agreed to go our separate ways.

Today we are still good friends. She knows me better than anyone and she remains my go-to person whenever I need someone to talk to. There was no malice during our separation, no petty arguments about who would have what. We simply decided between us what we wanted, and split the proceeds of the house sale down the middle.

When I hear of angry contentious separations, where two people who were once in love begin to tear lumps out of each other and communicate only through expensive lawyers, I despair, because it really doesn't have to be like that.

Relationships will sadly sometimes end, that is just the way it is. It is hard enough having to cope with a breakup without then getting into fights that ultimately no one will win. All this will do is add to the stress and trauma both of you are going through. There are no winners in a relationship breakdown, so you should not be looking at it in a win-lose competition situation. You should aim to part as amicably and in as pain-free a way as possible, because in the end that is what will serve you both best.

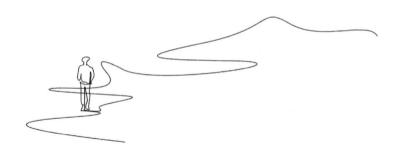

TAKING CHARGE OF EMOTIONS

In the first half of 2021, I found myself at the lowest point I had ever been in my life. My wife and I, who had been together for over thirty years, split up. When we agreed to separate, we put the large, four-bedroom family home up for sale and agreed to split the money straight down the middle. The house sold at the full asking price within days of going onto the market, and we both began to look for houses to buy for ourselves.

I quickly found myself a great place to buy and was due to move in once our sale was completed. Unfortunately, the seller turned out to be a complete nightmare—the paperwork wasn't forthcoming, deadlines were missed, and the seller's solicitor was completely incompetent—so much so that my solicitor put in a complaint. I ended up pulling out of buying the property.

Despite the purchase falling through, we still needed to sell our house to give my wife and I the funds we needed to buy our own properties. We set a deadline with our buyer for when the sale of the house would be completed. As the days went by and the sale date got closer, I still hadn't managed to find anywhere to live, despite my best efforts. Things had got so desperate that I was even considering moving back into my mum's house some

200 miles away from Bristol, where I had put my roots down.

At the last minute, my daughter managed to find me somewhere to live. It was an attic room in her friend's parents' house. I went to visit the room prior to accepting it and I found it to be extremely small and incredibly hot, especially in the middle of summer. But it was in Bristol and it wasn't my mum's. I accepted.

On the day of the sale, I moved into the attic room and my world became very small, literally overnight. I suddenly went from a big four-bedroom house with my own gym to living in a space with barely enough room to swing a very small cat in. I don't want to sound ungrateful, because I was far from ungrateful at the time. In my desperate need of a place to live, I was kindly offered the room, which got me out of the potentially worse situation of moving in with my mother back in Yorkshire. But to say I was left in shock and disbelief at the suddenness of everything would be a vast understatement. I felt like I was on autopilot, just dealing with every piece of shit and bad luck that seemed to be constantly flying in my direction. I was also asking myself how the fuck I had found myself in this position.

I felt worthless and very small, neither of which were factually true, but I was raw and my emotions were all over the place. I was desperately looking for something I could cling onto that would give me some sense of stability and hope whilst I rode out a storm that, at that time, seemed relentless and never-ending. I have always had a sense of pride in myself, but my ego was taking a major kicking as I was reduced to that small, rented room. *How the mighty have fallen,* I thought to myself.

Being a homeowner had given me a self-perceived status that I had not even been conscious of until I was suddenly no longer a homeowner. I realised what a privilege it is to own a property, to have the freedom to do what you wish, and wander around freely and unquestioned. Most of my possessions were now in storage and the few things I did take with me became very significant and important, as they were precious links to my past.

I found myself breaking down into uncontrollable tears over the slightest things. Objects as seemingly insignificant as a can opener I had brought with me would suddenly bring back a memory, and remind me of the home and family I had built and now lost. As the weeks passed by, I was beginning to feel like an even bigger failure for not being able to find myself a home to buy. The pity party I was throwing for myself was in full swing, with no end in sight. This made me feel even more useless and insignificant. Luckily, my friend Tony told me these feelings were not true. Tony told me very clearly that what I was going through was temporary; all of the feelings I had about myself were an inside job, and not the thoughts of others. He assured me that things would get better. In the end, he was proven to be right.

When you are in the middle of the storm, you often cannot see a way out; there is no end in sight, no sunlight to be glimpsed. My life during those first few months felt like complete chaos. I seemed to have no control over matters and the storm kept battering me as I desperately clung onto the life raft, just trying to survive from one day to the next, praying I could stay afloat long enough to reach the shore in one piece. I kept reminding myself what Tony had told me. *This is temporary.*

I had two hundred thousand pounds in the bank, just sitting there waiting to be used to buy a house. I joked at the time that I was probably the richest homeless man in Bristol. I put in offers for a further three houses, all of which fell through for various reasons and to my immense disappointment. Every time I found a potential new house, the initial feelings of excitement would give way to disappointment as the rug was pulled from under me again, and I would come crashing down onto the cold, hard floor of reality. It felt like the Universe didn't want me to move on. Maybe this was my karma for all the bad things I had done, and it was my time to payback my karmic debt.

At my lowest, I remember thinking, "If I go to sleep and never wake up again, it wouldn't bother me." In fact, it would be a relief to escape the pain I was going through.

I was fed up of feeling angry and hateful; I was just fucking tired of everything. But every morning I did wake up, thankfully, and because I woke up, I was given another twenty-four hours to fill.

After a few weeks, I managed to get my bike out of storage. The day this happened was a hugely significant and emotional moment for me, because having such a simple thing like my bike allowed me to escape the confines of my room for a few hours at a time and get out into the openness and fresh air of the countryside. This helped my mental health tremendously. My gym might have gone into storage for the moment, but I had got my bike back. It was like being reunited with an old friend.

I continued looking at a few more houses, but I was getting nowhere fast. I started to look further afield for property which I could afford and which ticked my requirement boxes. My search eventually led me to a lovely, detached, three-bedroom house with a garage and a nice garden within my price range. I put in an offer and told myself, if it is meant to be then it will be. My offer was accepted, and a few months later, I moved into my new home. As I write this now, I am in my front room with the sun shining through the windows. I have my gym and a lovely garden, which I plan to do some work on this summer. I have everything I need in life right now and I feel blessed. Looking back, I can see that the previous properties I had looked to buy were not meant to be, and I am grateful to have ended up right where I needed to be.

I had spent so much time and stress trying to buy property long before I eventually did. The Universe had been screaming at me to stop, but I hadn't listened and caused myself a whole lot of upset which I didn't have to go through. Ultimately, we have the choice to take on board or ignore the messages which the Universe sends us. If we ignore them, then we do so at our own peril, because in the end, what will be will be. Destiny prevails, regardless. You may ask, why bother doing anything if our life is already preordained? My answer to that is that the journey is part of the process; the adventure of getting to where we need to be is, in itself, the reward.

Since entering my fifties, I am beginning to learn the life lessons I wish I had learned many years ago. Had I done so, I am sure I could have saved myself countless years of stress, worry, and anger.

One of the biggest lessons now finally to be sinking in is the fact that we have control over how we think and react to people, situations, and events. We have control over our feelings and emotions, and we get to choose if we react with anger, hatred, or love. It was liberating to realise I didn't have to go down the path of anger and rage every time someone pushed my buttons. We have a choice whether we engage with thoughts of anger and then deal with all the negative consequences to our physical and mental health. We can also choose to observe feelings as they rise within us, but not engage with them. Look at it like being on a station platform; we observe the trains as they pass but we don't have to get onboard. These days, when negative thoughts rise within me, I try to become aware of them and just observe them. When I catch these emotions at their most embryonic of stages, I quickly remind myself that if I choose to jump onboard that emotional train then I will be caught up in its web for hours, days, or even months.

In the past, I would be completely overwhelmed and consumed by thoughts and feelings. I would find myself drowning in a sea of negativity, stress, and anger. I was the master at holding onto grudges, and by holding onto these grudges, others controlled me and my emotions. Often, I would find myself worrying about trivial issues; the smallest of things could play on my mind for long periods of time.

As humans, we can get caught up in cycles of negative thoughts and emotions. We have to be vigilant and constantly remember that we control how we think, we are in charge and not the emotion. Realising this simple fact was the "eureka moment" for me. My life became a whole lot easier when it sank in. That doesn't mean to say I don't fail, because I do, constantly, but I am getting stronger. I have a lifetime of bad habits and I still get caught out by my emotions. The difference now is that, when I see them rising, I try to catch them before it's too late, thus avoiding that downward journey of negativity.

HATE AND LOVE

It's fair to say I have at times been a very opinionated person. It pains me to admit this, but a lot of my life has been spent hating—actually, hate is a very strong word, so let's say disliking— be it people, music, fashion, politicians, famous people, etc. You name it—I have probably had an opinion on it. I spent so much time in an angered, bitter, and envious state because I felt inadequate in myself. I thought that by attacking others either physically or verbally, it would make me feel better about myself. It didn't , the reality was, the only person I damaged was me.

In my younger years, I had an irrational dislike of students. I personally haven't been to college or university, so I didn't know many students. The ones I did know or came into contact with seemed to be perfectly nice people. Even so, I always had an anger and dislike of students. I believed them to be snobs who looked down on the likes of me and thought of themselves as superior. As I analyse this today, I realise this dislike stemmed from the fact that I wanted to be a student; I was envious.

I wanted to be in that theatre of learning. I wanted people to see my intellect and not just view me as some worthless, working-class oik who had no future other than a prison cell or a lifetime on the factory floor. I wanted to be part of those debates around politics. Most importantly, I wanted to be heard and noticed. I wanted someone to see me for the genius I believed myself to be and save me from the life everyone else seemed to have me marked down for. (I feel I must explain that I am not so conceited to proclaim myself a genius, this was me from over 30 years ago.)

The irony of all this occurred when I fell for a student in the early 90s. I had travelled to Sweden and I was staying in a university hall of residence with an American friend of mine. Whilst there, I met a girl—another American student—who I fell for immediately. We both just clicked on an emotional and intellectual level. We ended up having a brief but beautiful affair before I had to return to the UK. On my return, the feelings continued and we kept in touch over the phone and through letters (no mobile phones or emails back then). She was everything up to that point I had dreamed and hoped to meet in a woman: intelligent, political, and pretty. She got me, and the fact that she liked my music was an added bonus. We seemed to connect immediately on every level, something I had never experienced before.

Unfortunately for me, she had a boyfriend back in America, which complicated matters. Looking back, it can't have been easy for her, having this crazy intense British guy just walk into her life and turn everything upside down overnight in the way that I did. (I hadn't gone to Sweden with the intention of falling in love. I had gone over with the intention of staying a few weeks with my mate, doing a few gigs to promote my record and getting pissed, but that all went out of the window within a few days of arriving.) It was clear she was torn between me and her boyfriend back home.

We remained in contact for a while, and the letters we wrote each other were long, heartfelt affairs. Mine no doubt reflected whatever self-pity and inner turmoil I was going through at the time. Our phone conversations lasted hours, and I desperately wanted to go back to Sweden to be with her. But she was still trying to deal with the emotional turmoil of meeting me and having the boyfriend back in America. I never did return to Sweden, and I eventually met and fell for someone else, who would later become my wife.

I did sometimes wonder what my life may have turned out like had I moved to America to be with the girl in question. Maybe I'd be talking with a slight American accent, drinking bourbon, and wearing a MAGA hat (trust me, the MAGA hat bit would never happen). But as I have alluded to many times in this book, things happen for a reason. Maybe our reason for meeting was purely to have that special someone whom we can tell anything to.

It is a human desire and need to feel that we are heard and noticed. We want to register with people; we want our existence to matter. All the anger, all the rage I felt was me screaming to be noticed and loved. Confronting the hateful and self-loathing person I was after all these years and writing it down is incredibly painful. It is not easy being this honest and reliving events and actions which you have buried deep within you for decades. Even throughout all the madness, there was always a better, kinder, and more loving man inside who desperately wanted to break out and be heard. A few people witnessed this man and could see through the bullshit exterior to the authentic me—my American friend being one of them. There was an inner me who would also be revealed in the brutal honesty of my song lyrics, which were also scathing of my failings. Listening back to those songs today, it is very clear that here was a man screaming out in pain and self loathing.

I penned the following song, titled "This Cross I Carry" in the early 90s. I think it captures the madness of my drinking and fighting and longing to be loved during that time perfectly:

This cross I carry has been too heavy for too long
I've dreamed a million dreams that all went wrong
I've fought too many fights
And I've drank to make things right
But the edge is getting nearer and I am sinking deeper

Don't say a word unless it's one I haven't heard
Whisper your name in the public house of shame
You're dangerous and cruel but forever I'm your fool
You still keep me waiting while inside I'm slowly wasting

I've never been the one to just let go
I've paid the price for hoping that you'll show
My only crime is love and I'll never get enough
But the edge is getting nearer and I am sinking deeper

Don't say a word unless it's one I haven't heard
Whisper your name in the public house of shame
You're dangerous and cruel but forever I'm your fool
You still keep me waiting while inside I'm slowly wasting.

If you wish to hear anymore of my music (mostly demos from my studio days), head over to Soundcloud and search for Hooligan Confession, or alternatively head to YouTube where you will find a few songs and a few very bad videos...That's the music plug over, onto the next chapter.

LEARNING FROM MY MOTHER

I can trace all the early chaos, anger, pain, and hurt I felt in my life back to one painful event in my early childhood. My father walking out of the family home when I was eight years of age tore my world apart overnight. From a very early age, I watched my mother fall apart in front of my eyes.

I witnessed her break down in tears more times than I care to remember, and each time I witnessed her breakdown, I was left traumatised and scarred, although I wasn't aware of the damage this was doing to me at the time. I watched as various boyfriends entered her life and then left, and I saw the aftermath of each of those broken relationships. I heard the sobbing coming from her bedroom; I saw the tears, and I tried to offer comfort and be grown up, telling her everything would be okay. I would console her as she cried and wailed. I witnessed things that no child should ever witness. A child should be shielded and protected from such adult things. I wasn't, so sadly, I had to grow up fast and I learned very quickly how painful the adult world could be.

I was thrown headfirst into the pain of adult relationships and it is only now, looking back in detail and unearthing those deep childhood memories that I can ask the question, "Is it any fucking wonder I went off the rails?"

I became wise in the ways of adult relationships before I should ever have been exposed to such things. I witnessed no joy in the relationships I saw, only pain and sorrow.

I was also very aware of the tight financial budget my mum had and I found myself worrying constantly about bills on top of all the other worries. I witnessed more than a child should ever see, and all before I had even started secondary school.

There seemed to be no attempt to hide any of these issues from me. My mother was also prone to extremely violent verbal outbursts and rages when I did something that she perceived to be wrong. Trivial matters were blown out of all proportion and would end in me sobbing uncontrollably, heartbroken and in complete fear.

One such incident that always comes to mind from when I was probably nine or ten years of age, is when I saved a bird from our neighbour's cat. I was at home upstairs when I heard a commotion outside. When I looked out of the window, I saw my neighbour's cat attacking a starling. I ran downstairs into the back yard, jumped over the garden wall, and saved the bird from the clutches of the cat. When I picked it up, I could see it was in a bad way and was clinging to life, so I brought it into the house. My mum was very superstitious, which was yet another load of paranoia and fear she placed on me. I was told to never pick up knives yourself which you had dropped, to throw any spilt salt over my shoulder, that breaking a mirror brings seven years of bad luck, and so on. There was even according to my mother, a superstition that bringing birds into the house would bring bad luck.

Sadly, the starling was too badly injured to be saved and died shortly after I had brought it inside. My mum came home, saw that I had brought a bird into the house, and began to rant.

"I told you never to bring a bird into the house. It's bad luck!"

She began to ramp up her screaming and shouting. I kept repeating that I was sorry but this had no effect on her relentless outburst. Eventually, due to her ranting, I began to sob. Even the sight of me sobbing didn't stop my mother from continuing with her onslaught. She was now getting completely out of control. Her rage went on for some considerable time and culminated in her throwing a shoe, which hit and smashed the living room window that looked out onto the back garden. My mum's words after smashing the window were: "See, I told you they bring bad luck."

I was now sobbing my heart out so uncontrollably that I could barely catch my breath. The bird had nothing to do with the smashed window or the uncontrolled rage my mother went into. This was all of her own making. She had the choice to react rationally or irrationally. She chose irrational, leaving her young son in an emotional mess and wondering what was so wrong about trying to save a small bird's life. It was an innocent act born out of compassion, but one which ended up being punished by an adult who had lost control of her emotions and her senses.

I would like to be able to say that this incident was a one-off, but sadly it wasn't. Her completely irrational rages could be triggered by any number of trivial things, and when this happened, I would often be left desperately sobbing.

At the age of thirteen, my mum brought yet another man into her life (and also into mine). This is the man I have previously referred to, whom my mother had two children with.

She had met him at work, and to win over my mum, he treated me okay at first. He had a car, which was something my mother didn't have, and he would take us on day trips to the seaside resorts of Scarborough and Bridlington. Not that long after being introduced to him, he moved into our home.

He was younger than her by nearly ten years, and he would go on to poison the relationship between me and my mother forever. I would hear him constantly attacking me verbally to my mum. It got so bad that I ended up living in my bedroom as I couldn't bear to be in the same room as him. He made it very clear he didn't want me around. He wouldn't even speak to me directly, and any messages were relayed via my mother.

With such a toxic person living under the same roof as me and him regularly verbally attacking me, my confidence became hugely damaged. I constantly received messages that I was bad, worthless, and not wanted. It is only within recent years that I have been able to reflect on my childhood, and begin to join the dots and see how these early experiences led to my later troubled and violent behaviour. I can also now understand why I no longer have a meaningful relationship with my mother.

I was once very close to my mum, and the thought of losing her as a child filled me with terror. If she was just a few minutes late getting home, I could be in floods of tears thinking the worst had happened. My dad had left me and the last thing I wanted was my mum to be taken away from me as well. It saddens me to think that we were once that close, yet now I have very little contact with her and can easily go well over a year without actually seeing her in person.

After my girls were born we would go to visit my mum on a regular basis. I began to realise that after each visit I would leave feeling upset, depressed, and angry. Visiting her was not a pleasure; it was more like a toxic activity which I had a duty to go through every few weeks. Both me and my wife spent many years trying to help and advise her on her problems, but to no avail. I was perpetually the adult advising her on her life. So much of my time and energy was being wasted on trying to help her, whilst at the same time I was trying to build my own life with my wife and our first daughter. I became exhausted by the same dramas which would play out at every visit.

In the end, I came to the realisation that she was never going to change. She would always find excuses and someone else to blame for her problems and misery. She would never take responsibility for anything which had happened. In her eyes, she was a victim and she was powerless to change anything.

In truth, she has always had the power to change anything she wished—we all have such power. As adults, we have complete control over our own lives. To solely blame others is a position of complete weakness. After a while, I tired of the negativity. I woke up to the fact that I didn't need such negativity in my life, or in the lives of my daughters. So I withdrew from my mother's life.

It was a lesson learned for me, that no matter how hard you try to help some people, they can never be helped, and you should cut your losses and bail out, or risk being dragged down with them, which is what I could see happening with my mum. To cut such people loose is not a callous act, but one of acceptance that you cannot change or help some people.

Today, we send the occasional text to each other, and I send her a birthday card, but I have no desire to visit and end up feeling the way I have done previously. I would like to be able to say that I miss her and that I feel sad, and maybe somewhere inside there is a sadness about how we have ended up like this. But I feel she let me down and failed me in so many ways that I am only now beginning to truly understand. As a child, you have unconditional love for your parents. I loved my mum, no matter how shit she treated me at times; she was my world. I feel I must say at this point that I know she loves me deeply—I am her son. Also, I feel

I have to be honest, because that is what this book is all about. Honesty, I have no real deep feelings for her these days. I have no desire to be in her company. I feel no hate or particular anger anymore; my feelings for her can best be described as neutral. I do feel sorry for her and how her life panned out. But it could have been so different, had she not let fear be the controller.

One of the main lessons I have learned whilst reflecting on my early life with my mother is that you need to be stronger than your fear, otherwise it will dominate and control everything you do, It will keep you stuck in whatever shit situation you are in.

No matter how shit and hopeless your life may seem, no matter how low and depraved your actions become, there is redemption to be had if you are truly looking for change and seeking a more peaceful life. We are all victims of the circumstances and traumas we experience particularly in early life. We carry these traumas around with us until they eventually start to leak out in various ways. My leakages of this internal toxicity manifested into violence, songwriting, drinking, and the abusing of others as well as myself. But redemption is available for all of us.

For me, writing this book is all part of the healing process and coming to terms with those events. It is also about forgiveness, forgiveness for myself, and letting go of the past.

It is an opportunity to unpack and expose the traumas that have haunted me for decades and, at the same time in doing so, hopefully help others see that they can survive, move on and live the life they want to live.

To move forward, you must acknowledge your traumas and face head on the demons they create within you. You must acknowledge the hurt you have caused others and confront all of the internal detritus which is holding you back and preventing you from moving on, because until you do the confronting, you will remain stuck in exactly the same place you find yourself in now.

An old friend of mine told me recently that he could always see the good person within me and knew that good person was fighting to get out and be seen. This person had witnessed me at my very worst. We all have the opportunity to redeem ourselves if we so wish. No one is a completely lost cause; whilst you are still breathing, there is opportunity to change.

FATHERHOOD

My greatest personal achievement in life has been my two beautiful daughters, now both adults in their twenties. Even now, it still blows my mind to think that I created and gifted two such beautiful, caring, and thoughtful people to this world. They are everything I was not in my youth, and the reason they are both so unselfish and compassionate towards others is down to me and their mum.

I must admit, when I learned I was going to be a father for the first time, as well as excitement, I also felt a lot of trepidation. It hit me like a thunderbolt; I was now going to have to be a real grown up. I had the responsibility of another human.

How would I cope with such responsibility?

Would I be able to cope?

Would I feel love?

The answer to all the above questions was, *Yes, I would.*

From the moment they entered this world screaming, my love was instant and I was aware of the massive responsibility I had to my daughters. Being present at both births left me feeling emotionally drained afterwards, and I remember returning home on my own after they were born, just lying on top of my bed and letting the enormity of what had happened sink in. My thoughts were many, too numerous to mention here, but I'm sure every fellow dad will know exactly how overwhelmed I was feeling during those first few hours following the births.

Having my girls was my chance to put something positive and good back into the world. I wanted them to have everything which I never had growing up. I wanted a stable, loving family home for them. From the very moment my eldest was born, everything I did was for them. They were the reason I stayed in shit, soul-destroying, stressful jobs. I wanted them to have all the chances and experiences I had never received.

I have always been honest with them both. They are both aware of some of my past. I have felt it is important that they know where I have come from, and some of the struggles I have faced.

I have told them of the good, the bad, and the ugly. And my message to them has always been the same as it has been constantly throughout this book. You can do and achieve anything, if you truly want it.

When my daughters became aware that as adults we have to work to earn money, I always told them that if they can get paid to do something they really enjoy, then they have hit the jackpot, because as we know, many people do jobs they do not particularly enjoy. I meet such people on an almost daily basis, which is why I have been so keen to push home to my girls to be brave, because nothing comes to those who have no plan and just exist.

Both attended dance classes from a very young age, and they took to dancing like ducks to water. This meant most weekends (and also a good few weeknights and school holidays) were spent taxiing my daughters to and from dance classes, shows, and competitions. I have spent literally tens of thousands of pounds on dancing lessons and shows for my wonderfully talented girls, and

I don't regret a single penny or minute of my time invested in it. Some of my proudest dad moments have been watching my daughters perform at numerous venues across the UK. Seeing them perform locally at the Bristol Hippodrome, Bath Theatre Royal, and the Redgrave Theatre were particularly proud moments for me.

My eldest daughter is now a dance teacher, getting paid to do something she loves. She runs her own very successful dance school, and is passing on her love for dance to the next generation. My youngest daughter is looking to follow in her big sister's footsteps. I could not have wished for two more lovely daughters. They are my gift to the world, which is a better place with them in it.

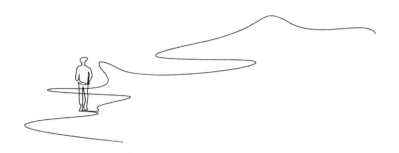

BREATHE IN THE UNIVERSE

Recently, I was privileged to find myself, along with four others, in the company of author and BAFTA award winner Geoff Thompson at Coombe Abbey. We spent a beautiful afternoon in deep conversation over tea, and Geoff spoke to us about his life, his work, and spirituality—which gave us all great inspiration. For me, it was an honour to sit at the same table as the great man once again, listening to him speak.

Geoff had a humble beginning, sweeping factory floors during the day in his hometown of Coventry. At night, he was a nightclub bouncer. He was a black belt in a number of martial arts, but was still held back in life by fear. By his own admission, he feared not only the physical, but life itself and its endless possibilities. Even so, Geoff knew there was more to life than sweeping the floors of a Coventry factory. He would often tell his workmates of his exploits as a bouncer, and this led to him eventually writing the stories down in a notepad by hand, whilst sat on the toilet at work. For Geoff, the moment his pen touched the paper of that first notepad, his whole life changed forever. Those handwritten words in those notepads became Geoff's first published book, *Watch My Back*, and since then, Geoff has written plays, films, over fifty books, and has won a BAFTA.

During my meeting with Geoff, he brought along the very notepads which went on to become *Watch My Back*. They were the proof that, no matter who you are or what your circumstances are, you can change your life. I was privileged to hold and read some of the lines written within those notepads over thirty years ago whilst Geoff was a factory floor sweeper. I was also able to hold the BAFTA he was awarded—more hard evidence. As Geoff has said, "Anything is possible. If I can write books and go on to win a BAFTA, as a factory floor sweeper and bouncer from Coventry, then you can do it. Just do the work."

And here lies the problem for most people: the work.

The work is uncomfortable, and discomfort is something we all naturally want to turn away from and avoid. But if we are to expand and grow, not just professionally, but also spiritually, then we need to be where the discomfort is; we need to sit and marinate within the discomfort, and take inspiration from it, knowing that this is where the growth is. And, of course, we must do the work; there is no success in any field without work. So many people want all the glory, accolades, and prizes, but don't want to do the hard work. They don't realise that to have the accolades without the work would be empty and meaningless. We all know how great it feels when we have worked really hard to achieve something. I remember as a child saving up all my money to buy records and books, and because I had saved up to buy them, they meant so much more than if I had done nothing, and had just been given them. So I repeat again: do the work, and watch your world change and expand.

Wherever you are in life right now is a result of everything that you have done up to this point in your life. If you are not happy where you are, then I want to you to know that, however old or young you are, change is possible. Redemption is possible. Happiness, peace of mind, and success are all possible. But only if you are prepared to lean into the sharp edges of discomfort and put in the work.

At this moment in time you may not really know what it is you want or are searching for. You may have a feeling deep within you that there has to be something more than just this.

In my twenties, what I thought I wanted and needed is very different to how I feel today. Back then, I wasn't really aware of how powerful the Universe is. I was unaware of how every day we are given clues and nudges by the Universe to where we need to be and what we should be doing. Spirituality was something which *weirdos* were into, and it was definitely not for someone like me. It is only in recent years that I have begun to have an understanding of how everything is connected, how every action has a reaction, and how powerful unseen forces are at play.

Yesterday, I went to the beach in the evening, when the crowds had largely disappeared. It was windy, the tide was in, and the sun was starting to set. I walked onto a stretch of beach which was largely deserted and stood looking out across the water. I saw the sun reflecting on the sea, the waves crashing, the wind blowing—and I felt the immense power of the Universe right there. No matter how powerful man thinks he is, he could not have stopped what I was stood in the middle of. I breathed it in deeply and thanked the Universe/God for the privilege of being given this life, which enabled me to experience the beauty and power before me. All this was free, the greatest free show on earth, so powerful and yet largely ignored. We get caught up so much in the trivial matters of our own lives that we miss these incredibly beautiful and powerful shows which happen every day right under our noses.

Take time each day to just stop, be quiet, and tune in to the Universe. You don't have to sit cross legged under a tree chanting a mantra (though a mantra can be extremely useful in focusing the mind), but take just five minutes to be aware of the Universe, and trust me—you will feel the benefits. Listen to your inner voice—that's God/the Universe talking to you. Learn to listen and to look for the signs and messages which are presenting themselves to you daily, they are your guide.

Invest in yourself—you are worth it. It is also an important part of the work which you must do to achieve your dreams. People think nothing of spending a few hundred pounds on fixing their cars, but they won't spend anything on fixing themselves. They go through life without ever truly investing in themselves. And when I talk of investing in yourself, it doesn't have to have a financial cost to it, it can be just taking some time out to sit in silence, alone and listening.

The most successful people on earth, from sports stars to business people, all invest in themselves. They hire coaches to help them on their journey. When they become successful, they continue to hire coaches to maintain and improve their performances. You can't expect to have success, in any form, without investing in you.

For years, I spent my life worrying about money, convincing myself I couldn't afford things, telling myself I didn't have enough, etc. I denied myself so much. The truth is, there is an abundance of money out there just waiting to be received, if not by you, then by someone else. In my own experience, I have always found the money I needed, when I needed it, and for whatever it was I desired. From holidays, to cars, and even houses—I would worry myself sick about affording these things. But once I fully committed to something, I found the money. The act of committing to something sets the wheels in motion for you to get moving, do the hard work, and create the necessary energy to pay for it. Until we commit, we sit at a standstill because we have no reason to move. Movement is the key, and committing will ensure you set yourself a goal to find a way to pay for it. And, yes, it might be scary, but, fuck me, it's also exciting. Show the Universe you are serious and the Universe will help and guide you.

I have recently been speaking with a friend. My friend is, by his own admission, presently in a dark place. A few months ago, he met a woman, fell in love, and quickly moved in with her, miles away from his family and friends. He reached out to me and said he was regretting this. He felt lost, depressed, unmotivated, and wanted to return home to where his daughter and grandkids are.

I told him he should go with his gut feeling, as that is often the truthful, inner voice screaming out from within you. We often fight our gut instincts and later regret ignoring them. How many times have you really wanted to do something, everything within you was saying YES, but then you let doubt creep in and take over, and before you know it you have convinced yourself not to do it? How many fantastic ideas and dreams have been quashed before they were even given a chance to live? I can think of a number of ideas I have had over the years, which I now look back on and wish I had done. One instance that comes to mind was pulling out of buying a second property. Had I gone ahead and bought that particular property, I would now be sitting on a very nice profit from my original investment.

Back to my friend; He knows what he needs to do, but is held back by guilt—something I know only too well. When I separated from my wife, I felt tremendous guilt for splitting up the family and having to sell the family home. I felt so much guilt for putting someone I still loved (but just couldn't live with any longer) through so much turmoil, and having to start again. What she was going through I was also going through, but the guilt I felt made it feel so much worse. It was the most difficult thing I have ever done in my life, but I went through with it and came out the other end still in one piece. What happened to me was meant to happen, and the Universe put me in the right place to learn a valuable lesson. I told my friend that he was exactly where he needs to be at this moment in time, as the Universe is giving him a lesson to be learned. Once it is learned and absorbed, then he can move on.

Sometimes we need to stop fighting. We have to surrender and go with the flow, let ourselves be directed and guided by the Universe. Often, that guidance reveals itself as our gut instinct. So don't ignore it, let it speak and listen.

TRIUMPH OVER INTIMIDATION

A couple of weeks ago, I went to a local store to buy a few things for my garden. As I was making my way to the checkout with my basket in hand, I heard a commotion by the exit door, though it wasn't obvious what was going on at first. I could see a male talking loudly and surrounded by other people. I then heard swearing and realised this was more than just a minor dispute, so I walked over to take a closer look and assess the situation. The young male, who appeared to be in his early twenties, had an item in his hand and was being prevented from leaving the store by a number of female staff. He was becoming louder and more threatening, claiming that he hadn't stolen anything and that he had come into the store with the item he now had in his hand—which, of course, was bullshit. There were male members of the public watching the commotion, but no one did anything to help the female members of staff who were being increasingly abused and threatened. I decided I needed to intervene to ensure the staff members weren't assaulted.

Putting my basket down, I walked over to where the commotion was and put up my fence, a self-defence stance where you have your hands in front of you to control the space and distance between you and an aggressor.

I told the lad to stop threatening the shop assistants. This quickly drew his attention away from them and onto me. He looked at me with his screwed-up, anger-filled face and screamed, "Why? What are you gonna do, bang me?" (hit me)

He saw that I had my left hand up in front of me and my right hand held back in a fist, ready to launch an attack if he entered my space. He also spotted the sweatshirt I was wearing, which featured a boxer and the name of the self-defence club I run. He continued to scream at me and the staff, so I warned him again to stop the threats. He loudly claimed that he had just come out of prison and he didn't give a fuck; this will have been done in an attempt to make me believe he was dangerous, and frighten me. It failed. He then asked me again if I was going to bang him. "That depends on you," I replied.

I knew he was all hot air; I had come across his sort many times before. He was hoping that by screaming and shouting, he could intimidate and get his own way. He had probably done this many times before against people he felt he could intimidate and who didn't understand the adrenaline dump. I'm sure previously all this noise will have worked, and he had probably managed to back people down and bully them until he got his own way, but not today. I could see how much of a fucking amateur he was when it came to the physical. His hands were down by his side, his chest was puffed out, and he was posturing—he didn't even realise he was offering me an open target to his head, which if I so wished, I could easily hit with full force and zero resistance, rendering him unconscious.

But I am a changed man these days and do not wish to hit anyone unless I have no other option than to do so.

What I tend to do with people who are being very aggressively loud is turn the volume down. I don't listen to the words, it's just noise. I fade the noise into the background and I do not focus on it. As I said, it is all designed to intimidate and scare you.

In my experience, people who are really going to attack you don't tend to give you a warning first. They tend to just launch an attack. It's a bit like burglars—they don't give you pre-warning that they are going to visit your house and break in. Most people who seriously want to attack you will just do it. So I always focus on a person's body language, their movements and actions.

Once I had turned down the volume of the loud, posturing young man who was before me, I could see he was actually an extremely scared individual. His loudness was an attempt to frighten and intimidate others, but was also masking his weakness and fear. After a couple more minutes of shouting threats at myself and the shop assistants failed to move any of us, he realised he had two options: he would either have to fight me or leave the store. He decided wisely and left, but not before throwing the goods he was attempting to steal down onto the floor in a final act of defiance. He then ran at the exit doors, barging past the ladies blocking his path. I followed him outside, where he proceeded to issue more threats towards me and the staff, before eventually disappearing.

When I went back into the store, I was patted on the back by watching members of the public. I asked the ladies if they were okay, knowing full well how they must be feeling after having had a massive adrenaline dump coursing through their bodies. I then picked up my basket and made my way to the tills, moving on with my day.

So what is the message to be had here? Don't be intimidated by the volume coming out of someone's mouth; turn it down and concentrate on their actions. Words will not physically hurt you, but actions will. Watch their movements.

Help someone if they are trying to stop an attacker, don't just stand there doing nothing. Support them, back them up. Only by good people coming together can we beat the bullies of this world. Simply sitting back and thinking, "It's not my problem," allows bullies to get away with intimidating and attacking innocent people. No one came forward to help me during this incident; they simply stood back and watched. As a society, we all have to collectively come together and help each other.

As the famous adage says: "The only thing necessary for the triumph of evil is for good men to do nothing."

NEGATIVITY IS AN INSIDE JOB

If we treated and thought about others as we treat and think about ourselves, it would likely disgust and anger us.

I am becoming increasingly aware of how we mentally torture and beat ourselves up on a daily basis. We put ourselves down constantly in ways that any enemy would be hard pushed to beat. We tell ourselves that we are not good enough: we are worthless, unlovable, undeserving, and useless. It is a constant stream of negative thoughts, messages and self-inflicted mental abuse.

If we were to witness someone expressing such negative messages to another person, we would be sickened and angry at what we heard. We would likely try to intervene and tell the abuser that what they are doing is wrong and unacceptable. Our compassionate instincts would encourage us to try and protect the victim. Yet, we do very little to protect ourselves from the internal abuse we subject ourselves to daily. We sit in silence as the negative thoughts and messages enter our minds. We listen and absorb the abuse in complete helplessness, becoming victims of our own inner voices. These uncontrolled inner voices bully us and chip away at our confidence, until one day we find ourselves hitting rock bottom. They can drive us to a breakdown, and in the very worst-cases, to self-harm or even commit suicide.

Hitting rock bottom is the worst place imaginable to be, but that is exactly where I ended up during the summer of 2021. At that point, my internal voice was telling me I was worthless, that my daughters no longer respected me, that I wasn't loved, and that things wouldn't get any better. I got to a point where I didn't care if I woke up in the morning. I was breaking down into uncontrollable tears at the smallest of things. I was in the middle of a very dark and fierce storm that I could see no way out of. In my mind, I had lost everything.

Being a fighter, I fought ferociously to be positive. I knew what I should be thinking and working towards. I had read countless self-help and motivational books and articles. I listened to hundreds of self-help podcasts. But in that moment, in the middle of the storm, nothing was connecting with me. For the first time in my life, I was at a complete loss.

Look at how you've lost everything: your family, your wife, your home. Look at how pathetic you are—reduced to living in a small, dark attic room owned by the parents of your daughter's friend. You are worthless, a failure, unlovable.

I couldn't escape the tirade of my inner voice. The Universe seemed to be against me. Every small chink of light I thought I saw was quickly extinguished and I would be plunged into darkness again. In the end, exhausted physically and emotionally, I stopped fighting and trying to control everything. I surrendered, handing my fate over to the Universe, or God, or whatever name you want to give it. I knew I had to hand over my predicament to a higher force and trust that what will be will be.

To surrender to a higher force can feel liberating. It allows you to remove the heavy burden you have been carrying on your shoulders and breathe again. It was only once I had surrendered that small but positive things began to happen—"little victories", as I call them.

I finally got my bike back out of storage, which allowed me to escape my room and get out into the fresh air. I could exercise and feel free again, and it was something I could control. It felt good to have something enjoyable from my old life back, and this small thing became a huge victory, lifting my spirits. Suddenly the world didn't seem quite so dark.

We have to go to war with those negative inner voices and not allow them control over us. They are the enemy within which must be defeated. It is a battle waged for sovereignty over the self.

Instead of telling yourself, "I can't," tell yourself, "I *can,* and I *will.*" Catch those negative thoughts as they enter the mind and fight against them with positive thought. Keep repeating the positive thought like a mantra, until the negativity is completely drowned out.

My friend Tony Somers gave me wise advice about dealing with negative thoughts during this time, and it has stuck with me to this day. He told me, "It's an inside job, Steve. None of it is true."

No war is ever easy; they are bloody and torturous. But we must remain focused on being victorious. We have to fight and ultimately silence those negative thoughts, and stop the self-defeating inside job.

You have got this far in life and survived, which suggests you are stronger than you probably even realise. So if you are going through a dark time, know that you will get through it and things will get better.

LIFE IS PRECIOUS

I believe that all life is precious and sacred, and we have no right to take the life of any other living creature.

I have been a vegetarian since 1987. In fact, I can even remember the very last time I ate meat. It was at a Leeds United FA Cup game at Swindon Town. (Leeds won 2-1, then went on to reach the semi-finals, which they regrettably lost to the eventual winners, Coventry City. Anyway, I digress.) I had already begun to eat a mostly vegetarian diet, but I was so hungry at the game that I relented and had a meat pie. Afterwards, I felt immediate guilt and shame, and vowed that would be the last meat I would ever consume.

Back in 1987, finding anything vegetarian was a struggle. The supermarkets didn't have the vast array of meat-free alternatives which they have today, and restaurants (especially fast-food outlets at football games) didn't have anything vegetarian other than chips, which were probably cooked in animal fat. Even so, it was and is something that I feel very strongly about.

During my time living in the countryside village of Poulshot, or "Poulshit", as I called it, I managed to get myself banned from the one pub in the village after attacking a fox-hunter, who with his mates had been boasting to me about his fox-killing escapades all night, despite me telling him to stop several times. When he went to the toilet I followed him and confronted him. With his mates in the bar he suddenly wasn't so boastful; anyway, I hit him, and as he fell back against the wall I hit him a couple of more times. Someone had heard the commotion, and with that the landlord came running in, grabbed me and told me I was barred for life. This was the very incident that led me to become a vegetarian. Fox-hunting was rather popular in the area, and the Duke of Beaufort's hounds would often pass my house on their way to the hunt. They would chase foxes to exhaustion and then the mounted human hunters would watch as the hounds ripped the fox to pieces in the name of sport. As they passed my house, I would shout abuse at the riders and followers from my bedroom window. I would also go out and make obstacles on the country tracks they used.

On a number of occasions, I confronted the followers who would watch the riders hunt from afar. It's fair to say I hated these people with a passion, and although I try not to hate anyone these days, I have to confess that it is still a struggle to not feel hatred towards someone who finds pleasure and delight in watching the organised abuse of a wild animal.

It is not a sport in any true sense of the word. Sport is a competition between two willing participants; the numbers are equal and both have a chance of winning. A fox being chased by dozens of hounds is not a fair contest, nor is someone with a high-powered rifle sneaking up on an unsuspecting animal and then blasting it through the head.

I had a love for wildlife from an early age. All creatures simply want to live their life, just like you and I. The way we as humans treat animals, especially those we farm for meat, saddens, sickens, and disgusts me. These are sentient beings who just want to live free from torture and pain, yet we treat them like worthless trash. Shoppers buy their nicely wrapped piece of meat from Tesco, not considering that it is the actual remains of what was once a living, breathing, feeling creature. They don't think about the terror that the animal felt as it was loaded on and then off the truck which transported it to the killing factory.

There is no difference between your pet dog, which harbours sheer joy and love for life, and a pig, cow, or sheep—other than its appearance. All living creatures have one desire, and that is to live. The animal whose flesh you consume felt terror, fear, and helplessness as it was kicked, prodded, and whipped. It didn't want to die. When you eat the body of an animal, you are literally consuming the complete terror at the point of its death as all those stress hormones are released and captured in its flesh.

Have you noticed how insects will scurry away, trying to find a hiding place when they feel threatened? Previously, when I have seen an insect in my house, I have often put my foot down and extinguished its life with no thought. Before you do the same, I urge you to watch the insect and see how it senses you and the danger it is in, how it tries to find safety, and literally runs for its life. You may feel its life is worthless and of no importance, but to that insect, its life means everything. All creatures, from the furry, cuddly types to insects, want to live, and who are we to play God and selfishly extinguish their life?

All life is meaningful and precious. I ask you to consider what has gone into producing the lump of flesh you eat. I ask you to consider humanely trapping that spider you find in your house and releasing it outside instead of thoughtlessly bringing your foot down on it. Every creature, whether big or small, has a place and purpose in this world, and every one of them is unique. There is no such thing as meaningless existence.

TRUST YOUR GUT FEELING

Have you ever entered a room, or met a person, or even walked down a street and had an inexplicable, uneasy feeling? Have you ever felt bad vibes or a bad energy about the situation? Sometimes, even though nothing has actually happened to you and no one is making a direct threat to you, you may instinctively feel that the situation is not good and that you should get out as soon as possible. When we get these feelings, we should not dismiss them.

For as long as I can remember, I have been able to sense potential danger and threats. On many occasions, I have been walking along a street with my wife or entering a bar when I sensed the need to leave, cross the road, or even turn around and walk back in the direction from which we came. In the early days of our relationship, my wife would look perplexed and ask why we needed to leave or go a different route. She eventually learned that when I said we needed to go, it was for a very good reason.

I can also instinctively sense if someone has a bad vibe about them and is best avoided. I sensed it with one of my daughter's ex-boyfriends. Immediately upon meeting him, I picked up that he couldn't be trusted and was not good for our daughter. I told my wife that there was something about him I didn't trust, and that I could see it when I looked into his eyes; his eyes literally showed me the darkness within him. I never said anything to my daughter, but I kept a close eye on events. Not long after I had told my wife what I had sensed, he and my daughter split up and the truth of how he had behaved came out. He was everything I had sensed and seen in his eyes. It didn't give me any pleasure to be proven right, as no father wishes to see his daughter emotionally hurt.

Another example was when I sensed straight away that the new boyfriend of a mutual friend was not all he claimed to be. On my first meeting with him, I just knew the story he was telling of his previous marriage and the cruelty and malice inflicted on him by his ex-wife was not true. I could sense that he was not a genuine and truthful person, and I knew he was not to be trusted. Unfortunately, my mutual friend was taken in and believed his stories. She eventually married and had two children with him. In the weeks before the birth of their second child, his true self was revealed and he disappeared seemingly from the face of the earth, leaving his wife to bring up two children on her own. As is always the case, the truth will out in the end. Everything I had sensed and suspected about the man was shown to be true.

There have been countless other instances in my life when I have sensed the true nature of a person. We all have the ability to tune into the energy and vibes around us and which individuals radiate. Everyone emits energy, and just as we can sense bad energy, we can also sense good, positive energies and vibes.

People will often describe parties and other gatherings as having a great vibe. I am sure you have all met people who give off such a positive and happy vibe that you have felt positive and happy yourself whilst in their company. There are people who can light up a room and who people seem to be naturally drawn to. Similarly, there are environments and people others want to avoid because they emit such a bad, dark, and negative energy.

As humans, we have this intuitive sixth sense within us, but rarely use it or take note of it these days. Wild animals rely heavily on it and constantly use it to stay alive. An animal can sense danger before they have even seen it. We no longer have to rely on this sense to stay alive, so for us, it has become a neglected instinct. Way back in time, when we were the hunted as well as the hunter, and we literally had to fight for survival, we were much more attuned to our sixth sense. To ignore it could have proved to be fatal.

If you have a dog, watch how it seems to sense things it cannot see. I have read reports of dogs being able to sense when their owners are nearly home. Though they may still be some distance from the house, the dog can sense they are on their way home. Dogs can also sense danger and they can even sense when you are ill.

We should tune into our natural senses more, and we should trust and act in accordance with what we are instinctively feeling. We have all heard the saying "Trust your gut feeling." Often, what our gut feeling is telling us is exactly what we should be listening to, trusting, and acting upon.

CHARITY

Lately, I see more and more videos on social media platforms of people filming themselves doing charitable things. In our increasingly social-media, celebrity-driven world, I'm sure you have come across countless videos of YouTubers randomly giving money to people who appear to be down on their luck. I have to admit that some of these videos I have watched have been quite moving. However, I also have an uneasy feeling about this trend, and often have to question if the act is done out of a genuine wish to help others or for the attention, clicks, and likes. If you are being truly selfless, then I believe you shouldn't be filming your act of kindness so you can post it on social media. That to me immediately begins to raise questions. I can fully appreciate the good feelings we can all get when we do something that helps others. But these acts should always be done selflessly, because you genuinely want to help. There should be no thoughts of boasting and reward. No looking to have our ego stroked, or praise from others. For me, posting your acts of charity and good deeds on social media screams that you are looking for attention. It suggests the act is really about you and not the person or cause you are helping.

George Michael, before his untimely death, was one of the most famous people in the world. After he died, it was reported that he gave millions of pounds to charities throughout his lifetime, under the strict instruction that his donations were not public knowledge. He didn't want the accolades and praise—his desire to help others came from a genuine place.

Today, we see so-called celebrities all too eager to be seen doing their bit for charity. They seem to be more motivated by the publicity it will gain for them than the actual cause.

There are numerous examples of this new breed of celebrity, who (whilst urging the general public to dig deep into their pockets) have later been exposed as actively dodging paying their taxes through complex tax-evasion schemes. Just imagine the good causes and public services which could have been helped financially if only they had paid their fair share of taxes? Personally I have little time for these shallow, self-obsessed people.

In the Bible, Matthew 6:1 says, "Beware of practicing your righteousness before other people in order to be seen by them, for then you will have no reward from your Father who is in heaven."

Do your charity and good deeds away from the eyes of others. Your charitable acts do not have to be particularly big. They could be something as simple as letting another driver out from a side road, or stopping to let a pedestrian cross the road. It could be picking up litter around your local area. Personally, when I go to the beach, if I see plastic I pick it up and put it in the bin. All these little acts of kindness collectively add up and make a huge difference. We can all do our bit and play a part, big or small, to make this world a kinder, more tolerant place to live. But do it quietly, don't broadcast and boast about it. Do it from a genuine place of love, and of wanting to help make a difference.

The rewards for you will come from knowing that your act of kindness has genuinely helped to make a difference. As they say, *It's nice to be nice.*

COURAGE TO LOVE

*"Those who have the courage to love,
should have the courage to suffer."*

—Anthony Trollope

One day you will fall in love. When I talk of love, I'm not talking about affairs which at the time seemed significant, but ultimately amounted to very little. I am talking about the kind of love that leaves a scar on your heart forever.

All relationships are meaningful in one way or another; they all happen for a reason, and we learn lessons from them all. Some relationships turn out to be much more meaningful and profound than others.

One day, if you haven't already done so, you will fall so deeply and insanely in love that everything you ever previously thought you knew about love will be turned completely upside down. It will be a love so intense and exciting that you are left feeling completely exhausted, overwhelmed, and confused, yet desperate for more. When you are in the middle of such a love you can think of little else. It is heaven and hell at the same time. All your insecurities will rise to the surface as you question if you are worthy and deserving of such love. It is complete madness, but, oh my—what a sweet madness it is.

This kind of love is so intoxicating that you never want it to end, but end it must, because no one can keep operating emotionally and physically at such an intense level forever. Our bodies and minds would not be able to cope—we would end up just breaking down and collapsing through emotional exhaustion. We hope the love we are experiencing will last forever; we hope with all our heart that they are the one with whom we will spend the rest of our lives with. We believe that no one else can ever make us feel like this.

The Greek philosopher Socrates summed up such love when he said, "The hottest love has the coldest end." Back in 1989, at the tender age of twenty-two, I met a girl who would become the first real love of my life. I will call the girl in question Jane (not her real name), and she was everything I wasn't. She was Australian, for one, and she was also a devout Catholic who took her faith very seriously. (Religion was something I was most definitely not into back then. It would be fair to say I was anti-religion, especially when it came to the Catholic faith and its views on celibacy, abortion, and contraception.) Jane came from a good, stable family, who, by my standards, were relatively wealthy. Our backgrounds and upbringing couldn't have been more different. To make things even more confusing, she wasn't even the sort of girl I would normally have gone for. Long blonde hair and an Aussie accent just weren't my thing.

After a drunken night out in a nightclub with friends, myself and Jane left the club and walked back to her place. When we got there, I was thinking, "I'm onto a certainty here," and feeling very confident, only to be firmly told that she wasn't the type of girl who dropped her knickers at the drop of a hat for someone she hardly knew, and certainly not on a first date. This left me feeling slightly shocked, but also strangely respectful—if not just a little sexually frustrated. Being the arrogant young man I could be back then, I wasn't used to girls saying no, especially when I had been invited back to their place. To me in 1989 being invited back to a girls place was as good as saying they were up for a night of passion between the sheets.

The next morning, we agreed to see each other again after she returned from a visit to Wales she had planned with friends. On her return, we began seeing each other often. At first, I saw her as just a stopgap before I met someone else, but over the coming weeks, before I even realised what was happening, I fell for Jane. I suddenly found myself actually missing her when we were apart. It also became apparent that Jane was starting to feel the same way about me. Before I really knew what was even going on, I was hook, line, and sinker in love—which scared the fuck out of me.

What I believed had been love previously soon paled in comparison to what I was now experiencing. Jane was the first girl with whom I felt safe enough to let my mask slip without fear of judgement or ridicule. She was the first girl I was able to open up to without shame or embarrassment, and who I allowed to break through that solid wall I had built around myself. I felt very vulnerable and exposed, and it petrified me to begin with. I was scared that she would leave me when she found out the truth about me and realised what I was. At that time, despite the hard exterior I portrayed to the world, I was extremely fragile, lacking in confidence, and scared. I was also very aware of my relatively poor upbringing in comparison to hers. She had travelled the world, and I at that point had barely left the shores of the UK. I didn't feel I was good enough for her.

Despite my best efforts of self-sabotage, she surprisingly stuck around, and my trust in her grew along with our relationship. We both experienced feelings that we had never experienced before for anyone else. Towards the end of 1989, what I had always feared happened: she returned to her native Australia and, despite our promises to be back together again soon, I knew in my heart it was over as we said our last emotional goodbyes at Heathrow airport.

We continued to have sporadic contact over the next few years, where we would declare our continued love for each other. But over time, the contact became less frequent until it eventually stopped completely. As the years passed, I presumed that, like me, she was probably getting on with a life of marriage and having kids. More years passed, and any thoughts about her faded into the distant recesses of my mind as I got on with being a husband and a dad.

For me, the relationship never really ended in the classic "we are finished" sort of way. It just fizzled out due to us being on opposite sides of the world to each other. Never having had a definitive ending to our relationship was something that always bothered me whenever I had a thought about Jane, not because I wanted to get back with her, but because I am a person who likes closure. It was like a wound that never had the chance to fully heal. On occasions when the drudgery of everyday life was getting me down, and I was struggling, I would sometimes think *what if*. What if I had got on that plane to Australia?

I would however quickly banish such thoughts, as dwelling on them did not serve me. I was now a married man with children, and my focus needed to be solely on my family not some long gone relationship.

In life, we have to keep moving forward. To live in the past is to miss out on the present. Believing that the past is where we were truly happy and thinking we can never experience such happiness again is to deny ourselves the wonderful life available to us now, which we all deserve.

Upon reflection, the time I spent with Jane—which I remembered as a joyous and happy time through my rose-tinted glasses—was actually a confusing and often painful time for me. When I began reading my diary from 1989 for the purposes of this book, it became blatantly obvious to me that I had been anything but truly happy. I was drinking heavily, hugely aggressive, and very angry at the world. I was also paranoid, massively insecure, and, emotionally, I was all over the place. Reading those diaries told a story of a young man who was lost and whose life was in total chaos.

Our memories, when we look back, seem to have a way of blocking out all the bad things which happened during what we believe to have been our happy times. As glorious and happy as the past may appear to have been, you can never relive it. It was of its moment and time moves on.

Do not wallow in thoughts of the past, because that prevents you from appreciating the great times you are currently living in. If you find yourself starting to be immersed in thoughts of the past, then try to catch yourself and bring yourself back to the present. We have to let go of the past and seek peace and happiness in the here and now.

Your first love will always be your first love; that is a fact. But they do not have to be your last love. Take it from me, you can and will find love again with somebody else who is more worthy and appreciative of your love.

To fall in love takes courage, you are entrusting your heart and emotions in the hands of another, hoping they will care for them, treat them kindly and with respect. Have no regrets if that love should sour, for you will have learned valuable lessons from it. You will know more about yourself and what you are prepared to tolerate, and, more importantly, what you are not. It will take time for the wounds of a broken first love to heal, but heal they will, and like every adversity which you face and overcome, you will be stronger for it.

REVENGE

I do not feel the world needs yet another violent book, so I have deliberately not written too much about the violence I have been involved in over the years. My history of violence is not something I am proud of, but I acknowledge it is something I cannot ignore completely and pretend never happened. The violence, the anger, and the rage all made me who I am today—which is someone now very opposed to and repulsed by violence.

One event in particular from my past taught me a very valuable lesson. I was in my early to mid twenties, living in Bath with my then girlfriend, later my wife. It was a late, midweek evening, and I was lying in bed when I received a phone call from someone I knew and was kind of friendly with. He rang me quite close to pub closing time, which was 11p.m. back when this occurred. He told me he was in the pub across the road from where I was living and said I should come over for a drink. I politely explained that I was already in bed and falling asleep. Clearly drunk, he kept telling me to get over the road to the pub, becoming quite abusive when I told him I wasn't coming out. I repeated that I was in bed and tired. He still didn't accept this and became more abusive towards me, so I put the phone down. I lay in bed, now fully awake, and became pissed off and angered when I thought about what he had said. How dare he fucking ring me up and abuse me like that?

My anger was such that I wanted to confront him about his call. I jumped out of bed, got dressed, and headed across the road to the pub where he was. I opened the front door of the pub and saw him at the bar with a couple of other lads I didn't know. After calling his name to get his attention, I began to tell him he was out of order calling me and shouting abuse down the phone. His mates became involved, so I told them to fuck off as it had nothing to do with them; I was then pushed out of the front door of the pub and onto the street.

In hindsight, I maybe should have left it at that. But I was now more angered and aggrieved, and wanted to let them know, so I entered the pub again. Before I even had the chance to say a word, I was rushed and pushed out of the door by his two friends and the barman, who had always appeared to fancy himself as a bit of a hard man. The barman was a stocky lad in his mid twenties, and this was the perfect opportunity to prove himself to be that hard man he believed he was—with the help of two others, that is.

I was pushed out onto the street, faced with all three of them trying to physically attack me. Funnily enough, Mr. Abusive had stayed in the bar. Punches and kicks were being thrown at me by the three brave warriors. I kept my hands up and I tried to maintain my distance whilst looking for an opening to get a shot in, but with three people all moving towards me, I ended up being backed off. I found myself pushed back into a nearby shop doorway, which was to be my undoing. Now I was cornered, with no means of creating distance or escape. Despite my best efforts at fighting back, I became overwhelmed by the punches and kicks of my three assailants and I took a bit of a beating.

After the attack had finished, I got back to my flat and went to the bathroom to look in the mirror and assess the damage. I had a few bruises starting to appear and some superficial damage to my face. My girlfriend, who had been asleep in bed next to me when I took the call, was now awake and came to see what I was doing. Upon seeing my damaged face, she became upset, shocked, and angered at what had happened to me; she got the first-aid kit out and began to clean me up.

As I lay in bed that night, I was unable to fall asleep as my head filled with anger and thoughts of revenge. I had been sinned against on this occasion, I told myself. I had received an abusive phone call, and I was sure the fuckers who jumped me were nothing on their own. They had taken a massive liberty by attacking me three to one. I vowed I would pay back every single one of them for their attack.

The next day, I woke early, and the first person on my list for a revenge visit was my now ex-friend who had made the call. He worked at a local newsagent, so I knew he would be there early in the morning to take delivery of the papers.

Just after 7a.m., I took a walk down to the shop where Mr. Abusive worked, wearing a coat which concealed a baseball bat I had tucked inside. When I arrived at the shop, I waited outside for the customers to leave before I entered. I closed the shop door behind me and flipped the Open sign so it showed Closed. Pulling out my baseball bat from under my coat, I approached the counter where Mr. Abusive stood with a look of terror in his eyes. I raised the bat above my head and smashed it down hard onto the counter, shouting, "You ever fucking speak to me like that again and this will be wrapped round your fucking head. Don't you ever ring me again, don't talk to me, and if I walk in a pub you're in, you fucking walk straight out or I will come for you. Do you understand?"

Oh, he understood alright, and I witnessed the colour drain from his face. I managed to keep my rage controlled enough to get the information I needed about the two lads he was with who attacked me. I already knew the barman."Give me the fucking names of those two cunts you was with last night," I demanded.

The names were given quickly and without hesitation.(I guess he felt he didn't have a lot of choice, given the fact he had a raging madman wielding a baseball bat within a few feet of him.) I demanded their addresses as well. He claimed he didn't know where they lived, but gave me one of their workplaces—a pub a few miles outside of Bath. He didn't know much about the other lad at all, as he was a mate of the one who worked in the pub. As I left the shop, I reminded Mr. Abusive what would happen if he should ever cross my path again.

My plan was to scare the shit out of each one of the cowards who had attacked me by turning up at either their places of work or their homes. Next on my list: the barman.

A few hours later, when the pub where I had been attacked opened, I entered to find him. As he saw me walk through the door, he appeared nervous. He knew I wasn't there for a friendly chat.

"Come outside now, I want a word," I demanded. I could see the fear in his eyes as he looked at me from behind the bar. He had been ever so brave the previous night with two others backing him up. Now, on his own, he wasn't so keen to leave the safety of the bar and come outside for a chat.

He made an excuse that he couldn't leave the bar, but I insisted that we needed to talk now. Knowing I wasn't going anywhere until this issue had been dealt with, he offered to speak in a small area just behind the bar, but with the door open so he could see the customers. *Fucking coward*, I thought, but reluctantly agreed, as I really didn't feel like dragging him outside, especially with witnesses present. I went behind the bar, where he tried to offer me a drink, hoping he could buy my forgiveness. But my forgiveness wasn't for sale.

The now not-so-brave barman was told, in no uncertain terms, what I would do to him should he ever cross me again.

"I know where you work. I know what time you leave. I know where you live. If you ever cross me again, I will come for you and put you in fucking hospital, is that fucking clear?" I asked.

Sheepishly, he nodded his head and even muttered an apology. With my second warning issued, I left the pub. Two down, two more to go.

That night, I made my way to the country pub where one of the remaining two attackers worked. I parked up in the car park so I could see the entrance to the pub and waited for closing time, with my baseball bat beside me on the passenger seat. Closing time came and went, and I was beginning to wonder if my previous night's attacker was actually working, when he finally appeared, walking out of the side door and towards his car. I grabbed my baseball bat and approached him. He was now sitting in his car and hadn't seen me coming towards him. I announced my presence by banging on the driver's side window. He looked round, startled to see my face close up to the window.

"Remember me, wanker?" I asked. Stupid question, really; of course he remembered me. He had been trying to smash my head in with two other cowards just the night before.

"Get out of your fucking car, ya cunt," I ordered.

"What do you want?" he asked, as if he didn't know that the baseball bat which I was now brandishing meant for him.

"I want a fucking word with you about last night, twat."

He wound his window down a few centimetres, but wouldn't open his door. I didn't give him a chance to try justifying his cowardly three-on-one attack, and I went straight into letting him know what I was going to do to him.

"You have no fucking idea what you fucking bit off last night, but I'm gonna tell you now. I know where you work and where you fucking live." I was lying about knowing where he lived, of course, but he didn't know that. "If you ever cross my fucking path again, I will come find you, either here or at your home, and wrap this fucking bat around your head. Now, you tell that to your fucking mate as well."

He didn't say a single word, just nodded to let me know the message had been understood. Clearly, this was yet another coward who didn't fancy getting physical on his own. The bravery he showed when the numbers favoured him had disappeared.

"Now fuck off," I told him. My work was done. A message had been delivered in person to all but one of my attackers, though I was certain the last one would be given the message.

My actions were very deliberate psychological messages designed to instill fear into each of them. I couldn't let them just walk away after their attack on me, with no comebacks. That would leave me at risk if they believed they could attack me again, and next time I might come off worse than just the superficial bruises I had suffered the first time. I needed them to think I was unpredictable and dangerous. They had to believe that I was someone who would happily turn up at their place of work or home seeking revenge. I also knew that this would be passed onto others.

If people think there is a possibility that you will bring trouble to their own doorstep, they tend to think twice before getting into another conflict with you. Our homes are the place where we feel most secure and safe; they are our sanctuary from all the madness that goes on outside. To have someone turn up on your doorstep is a violation of that sanctuary and safety.

I tell this story not to be boastful or glamorise violence in any way. Though I didn't use any actual physical violence, I knew that my threats would cause more fear and sleepless nights than if I had resorted to physical violence. I am not proud of how I was back then, and that person is not the person who is walking this earth today.

I can now also see that I didn't have to put myself in a position where I was attacked in the first place. I'm not saying I deserved what happened, but had I been in control of my ego, I would have just stayed at home in bed and not gone looking to confront Mr. Abusive in the pub, thus avoiding everything that followed.

I am on a peaceful path now, and I try to avoid confrontations at all costs. However, I know that deep within me there is still the potential to be that man again should I be sufficiently provoked. Today, the violent man I was would only ever be unleashed if someone were to threaten or hurt my family. I am not interested in lowering my frequency and wasting energy on parasitic people who, if allowed, would drain me of all my positivity. And believe me; I am tested frequently by low-energy people. It can be a battle at times to not allow myself to be dragged into their dramas.

Choose your battles wisely; ensure any battle you fight is worthy. In this case, at that time in my life and being the way I was, it seemed a worthy and just fight. I remember feeling quite proud of myself afterwards that I had not resorted to actual physical violence.

Today, for me this would not be a worthy fight. Yes, the phone call would piss me off still, but I would not go out actively seeking to right the wrong.

There will be people who you come into contact with who are

ignorant, rude, and confrontational. They will push your buttons and test the very limits of your patience, but it is important to realise that you will never change these people. Resorting to physical violence may give you a sense of satisfaction, but this will be short-lived and may well have serious consequences. These people, I am afraid, walk amongst us.

A good friend of mine gave me the following explanation and advice regarding such people: "They create anger within you because you are judging them by your own high standards and morals; remember, not everyone has the same standards as you, so stop judging others by that measure, otherwise you will forever be left disappointed."

Violence should only be used as a last resort, when all other options have been exhausted.

In the past, as I have freely admitted I have not always lived by this rule. But I have learned from my mistakes, and now, as a self-defence instructor, I make it very clear to those I teach that there is no such thing as good violence. All violence is ugly and has repercussions. Real life violence is not the glamorised portrayal you see on TV or at the cinema. On the street there are no rules and there are no referees to ensure fair play and a good clean fight. This is why I advocate so strongly that you avoid the use of violence at all costs. That said however, I believe that the use of violence can be justified if an attack on you or a loved one is imminent; in that moment I teach to strike first with ferocity until the threat is neutralised.

I believe that karma has no quarrel with you under those circumstances. You have not sought or asked to be in a situation where you are being threatened with physical violence; therefore the use of violence to defend yourself is in my eyes justified, not just from a legal stand point but also on a karmic level.

GOOD DAYS, BAD DAYS

The simple reality of life is you will have good days, and you will have bad days.

The aim for us all should be to have more good days than bad as we journey through this life.

There will be days when you wake up full of excitement, ready to face the day ahead with vigour and courage. Those are the days you feel invincible and full of belief that anything is possible. For me when I have these days, I feel totally connected to the whole universe, I walk with a spring in my step and have complete conviction and certainty in everything I do. It is truly a magnificent feeling and a natural high for me.

Then of course there are the bad days where you don't even want to get out of bed, the alarm goes and you just want to pull the duvet back over your head, and stay there all day. You don't want to see or speak to anyone. You struggle to see the positives in anything, and any small problems or issues that arise seem like huge insurmountable mountains.

Everything anyone does can seem like a personal attack on you. Your whole world can just seem to be caving in around you.

What I want you to know is, if you are having a bad day, we

all have them.

It is perfectly natural to feel this way. Even someone as seemingly cheerful as Timmy Mallett will have bad days when he probably just wants to shout "FUCK OFF" to the world.

But as I have said previously in this book, it shall pass. Nothing is forever, and another day will dawn, and life will again seem wonderful, and full of possibilities.

So hang on in there, be brave, things are never as bad as they may seem, and know and believe that you have got this.

In a world of eight billion people remember, you are wonderfully unique, there is no one else like you, and nor shall there ever be.

THE JOURNEY CONTINUES

L ife is a journey filled with endless lessons along the way. We
either learn those lessons, or we continue to ignore them at
our peril and make the same mistakes over and over again until
we finally learn and understand. Only then can we move on to
the next chapter.

People enter our lives for a reason. They may stay for only a
fleeting moment, or they may stay for many years, but all enter
for a purpose. That purpose may not be immediately obvious,
and sometimes it is only when we look back that the reason they
came into our lives becomes clear. Harbour no regrets about
anyone who has entered your life, not even those who you may
feel have impacted it negatively. Everyone taught you valuable
lessons and helped you grow and develop as you moved through
this life. Even the most negative of experiences can become our
teachers. For me, these negative events show me what I don't
want. Negative people show me how I don't want to succumb to
feelings such as hatred, selfishness, and anger.

We are all victims of our past, but we do not have to let our
past define our future.

It has been, at times, a painful journey for me to recall some of the battles and challenges I have endured, but it has also been extremely cathartic. Remember that everything happens for a reason, though the reasons may not be immediately obvious.

I hope this book helps you along your journey.

ABOUT THE AUTHOR

Permanently expelled from school at 15, and written off by his teachers, Steve was determined to prove his detractors wrong. He went on to realise his dream of becoming a singer/songwriter, releasing two records in the 1980s and appearing live several times on TV and radio.

Although periods of his life have been chaotic and violent, he now finds himself on a more peaceful path, mentoring, teaching self defence and writing.

Lessons Learned Without a School is Steve's first step into the literary world.

To find out more about the self-defence classes; 1-2-1 training and mentoring sessions that Steve holds in Bristol, you can visit the Real Combat System South West Facebook Group; or www.realcombatsystemsouthwest.com

Printed in Great Britain
by Amazon

44775660R00118